Convergence

Facilitating Transdisciplinary Integration of
Life Sciences, Physical Sciences,
Engineering, and Beyond

Committee on Key Challenge Areas for Convergence and Health

Board on Life Sciences

Division on Earth and Life Studies

NATIONAL RESEARCH COUNCIL
OF THE NATIONAL ACADEMIES

THE NATIONAL ACADEMIES PRESS
Washington, D.C.
www.nap.edu

THE NATIONAL ACADEMIES PRESS   500 Fifth Street, NW   Washington, DC 20001

This project was supported by the Raymond and Beverly Sackler Science Fund of the National Academy of Sciences, the Burroughs Wellcome Fund, the Kavli Foundation, Research Corporation for Science Advancement, the National Science Foundation through grant PHY-1353249, the National Institutes of Health through award HHSN263201200074I/HHSN26300047, TO#47, the William R. Kenan, Jr. Institute for Engineering, Technology & Science of North Carolina State University, the Frank Hawkins Kenan Institute of Private Enterprise of the University of North Carolina at Chapel Hill, and the Connecticut Institute for Clinical and Translational Science at the University of Connecticut. The views expressed herein are those of the authors and do not necessarily reflect the views of the organizations or agencies that provided support for the project.

International Standard Book Number-13:   978-0-309-30151-0
International Standard Book Number-10:   0-309-30151-3
Library of Congress Control Number: 20141940815

Additional copies of this report are available for sale from the National Academies Press, 500 Fifth Street, NW, Keck 360, Washington, DC 20001; (800) 624-6242 or (202) 334-3313; http://www.nap.edu.

Suggested citation: NRC (National Research Council). 2014. *Convergence: Facilitating Transdisciplinary Integration of Life Sciences, Physical Sciences, Engineering, and Beyond*. Washington, DC: The National Academies Press.

THE NATIONAL ACADEMIES
Advisers to the Nation on Science, Engineering, and Medicine

The **National Academy of Sciences** is a private, nonprofit, self-perpetuating society of distinguished scholars engaged in scientific and engineering research, dedicated to the furtherance of science and technology and to their use for the general welfare. Upon the authority of the charter granted to it by the Congress in 1863, the Academy has a mandate that requires it to advise the federal government on scientific and technical matters. Dr. Ralph J. Cicerone is president of the National Academy of Sciences.

The **National Academy of Engineering** was established in 1964, under the charter of the National Academy of Sciences, as a parallel organization of outstanding engineers. It is autonomous in its administration and in the selection of its members, sharing with the National Academy of Sciences the responsibility for advising the federal government. The National Academy of Engineering also sponsors engineering programs aimed at meeting national needs, encourages education and research, and recognizes the superior achievements of engineers. Dr. C. D. Mote, Jr., is president of the National Academy of Engineering.

The **Institute of Medicine** was established in 1970 by the National Academy of Sciences to secure the services of eminent members of appropriate professions in the examination of policy matters pertaining to the health of the public. The Institute acts under the responsibility given to the National Academy of Sciences by its congressional charter to be an adviser to the federal government and, upon its own initiative, to identify issues of medical care, research, and education. Dr. Harvey V. Fineberg is president of the Institute of Medicine.

The **National Research Council** was organized by the National Academy of Sciences in 1916 to associate the broad community of science and technology with the Academy's purposes of furthering knowledge and advising the federal government. Functioning in accordance with general policies determined by the Academy, the Council has become the principal operating agency of both the National Academy of Sciences and the National Academy of Engineering in providing services to the government, the public, and the scientific and engineering communities. The Council is administered jointly by both Academies and the Institute of Medicine. Dr. Ralph J. Cicerone and Dr. C. D. Mote, Jr., are chair and vice chair, respectively, of the National Research Council.

www.national-academies.org

v

Preface

The scientific opportunities enabled by convergence—the coming together of insights and approaches from originally distinct fields—will make fundamental contributions in our drive to provide creative solutions to the most difficult problems facing us as a society. This convergence provides power to think beyond usual paradigms and to approach issues informed by many perspectives instead of few. In my own experience, the potential for innovation and successful problem solving becomes greater when we are able to harness the knowledge bases, skill sets, and diversity of experience of individuals in an environment that fosters dialogue and respectful participation by all team members. Ultimately, I believe this will entail partnerships at the intersection not only of the life and medical sciences, physical sciences, computational sciences, and engineering, but also economic, social, and behavioral sciences, arts and humanities disciplines, and beyond, thereby amplifying the potential for innovations of incredible variety and magnitude.

Those who participate in convergent science are excited by the possibilities, but they know how difficult are the challenges to creating and sustaining environments that facilitate it. The present study was undertaken to better understand these challenges and to explore examples of current convergence programs in order to inform investigators and organizations interested in expanding or establishing their own efforts. Beyond this goal, the approach embodied by convergence provides a framework for thinking about the research enterprise and the network of partners that together form the ecosystem that enables science from innovative research to translational application. Convergence provides us with an opportunity not only to discuss strategies to advance science but also to elevate discussions on how to tackle fundamental structural challenges in our research universities, funding systems, policies, and partnerships.

I was joined in this project by committee members who enthusiastically brought their creativity and knowledge, informed by multiple areas of expertise, to the study, and it has been a great pleasure to work with each of them. We were also fortunate to have the support of the presidents of the three Academies—the National Academy of Sciences, National Academy of Engineering, and Institute of Medicine—in supporting a role for the National Research Council to address this topic. The committee's data-gathering workshop likewise drew on the contributions of scientists from graduate students to senior deans, along with agency, foundation, and industry leaders. Their perspectives were critical to the committee's thinking and I am grateful for their active engagement. Finally, on behalf of the committee, I want to recognize the dedication of the NRC staff, especially study director Katherine Bowman, who worked alongside us to bring the report to fruition. Their guidance, ideas, and support throughout the process were invaluable.

Bringing together the insights enabled by rapid progress across multiple disciplines has the potential to transform science for the benefit of society. It is the committee's hope that the report will bring awareness of this convergence to a wider range of audiences and stakeholders and catalyze the systematic efforts necessary to harness its power most effectively.

Joseph M. DeSimone, *Chair*
Committee on Key Challenge Areas for Convergence and Health

Acknowledgments

This report has been reviewed in draft form by individuals chosen for their diverse perspectives and technical expertise, in accordance with procedures approved by the National Academies' Report Review Committee. The purpose of this independent review is to provide candid and critical comments that will assist the institution in making its published report as sound as possible and to ensure that the report meets institutional standards for objectivity, evidence, and responsiveness to the study charge. The review comments and draft manuscript remain confidential to protect the integrity of the process.

We wish to thank the following individuals for their review of this report:

Ann M. Arvin, *Stanford University*
Michael M. Crow, *Arizona State University*
Jerry A. Jacobs, *University of Pennsylvania*
Philip M. Neches, *Teradata Corporation*
Jack C. Schultz, *University of Missouri*
Esther S. Takeuchi, *Stony Brook University*

Although the reviewers listed above have provided many constructive comments and suggestions, they were not asked to endorse the conclusions or recommendations, nor did they see the final draft of the report before its release. The review of this report was overseen by **William**

H. Press, *University of Texas* and **Robert H. Austin**, *Princeton University.* Appointed by the National Academies, they were responsible for making certain that an independent examination of this report was carried out in accordance with institutional procedures and that all review comments were carefully considered. Responsibility for the final content of this report rests entirely with the authoring committee and the institution.

The committee also thanks all those who participated in the workshop "Key Challenges in the Implementation of Convergence," held September 16-17, 2013 (Appendix B).

Contents

Boxes, Figures, and Tables

BOXES

FIGURES

TABLES

Summary

Convergence is an approach to problem solving that cuts across disciplinary boundaries. It integrates knowledge, tools, and ways of thinking from life and health sciences, physical, mathematical, and computational sciences,[1] engineering disciplines, and beyond to form a comprehensive synthetic framework for tackling scientific and societal challenges that exist at the interfaces of multiple fields. By merging these diverse areas of expertise in a network of partnerships, convergence stimulates innovation from basic science discovery to translational application. It provides fertile ground for new collaborations that engage stakeholders and partners not only from academia, but also from national laboratories, industry, clinical settings, and funding bodies. The concept of convergence as represented in this report is thus meant to capture two closely related but distinct properties: the convergence of expertise necessary to address a set of research problems, and the formation of the web of partnerships involved in supporting such scientific investigations and enabling the resulting advances to be translated into new forms of innovation and new products.

Knowledge created by the process of convergence can contribute to

---

[1] Throughout the report, the term "physical sciences" is commonly used as shorthand to include fields such as physics, chemistry, materials science, and the mathematical and computational sciences.

- understanding complex biological systems such as the nervous system and applying that understanding to design new medical treatments;
- improving patient outcomes through integrated knowledge management and precision medicine;
- revolutionizing manufacturing through advances such as on-site, three-dimensional printing;
- creating new fuels and improved energy storage systems; and
- meeting the world's need for secure food supplies in a changing climate.

The approach to research embodied by convergence is not the only way to advance knowledge or to work within and across disciplines. Research undertaken through other modalities or that addresses core problems not at interfaces of life, health, physical and engineering fields all provide critical contributions to the research enterprise. The results of such research also provide a wealth of knowledge that can be drawn on and recombined within convergence efforts. An example to illustrate the type of research challenge that would benefit from a convergence approach is presented in Box S-1.

Many institutions are interested in how they can better facilitate convergent research. Despite the presence of established models (Table S-1), however, cultural and institutional roadblocks can still slow the creation of self-sustaining ecosystems of convergence. Institutions often have little guidance on how to establish effective programs, what challenges they might encounter, and what strategies other organizations have used to solve the problems that arise. The present study was undertaken to address this gap. It aims to explore mechanisms used by organizations and programs to support convergent research and provide informed guidance for the community (Box S-2). A data-gathering workshop held in September 2013 provided an opportunity for members of the community interested in convergence to explore several key questions: What is enabled by convergence? What are the typical challenges encountered when nurturing it? What mechanisms can be used to support and facilitate convergent research? This workshop and the development of the present report were supported by a diverse array of sponsors who reflect the broad audience interested in discussing and understanding the challenges to implementing convergence effectively.[2]

[2] The project was supported by the Raymond and Beverly Sackler Science Fund of the National Academy of Sciences, the Burroughs Wellcome Fund, the Kavli Foundation, Research Corporation for Science Advancement, the National Science Foundation through grant PHY-1353249, the National Institutes of Health through award HHSN2632012000074I/

BOX S-1
Engineering the Microbiome to Treat Disease: A Challenge that Requires Convergence of Expertise and Partnerships

The human microbiome is the vast community of microorganisms that live within us, including on our skin and within our gut. Large-scale efforts to identify these microbes and correlate them with states of health and disease are under way, such as the Human Microbiome Project supported by the National Institutes of Health. By understanding the microbiome and microbial community interactions, it may be possible to develop therapies that harness altered versions of critical microbial components. For example, researchers recently engineered a commensal gut bacterium to produce a signaling molecule that causes the pathogen *Vibrio cholerae* to reduce its expression of virulence factors such as cholera toxin. When mice ingested the engineered bacterium prior to infection with *Vibrio cholerae*, they showed decreased toxin binding and increased rates of survival (Duan and March 2010).

The challenge of associating a particular microorganism or combination of microorganisms with a specific disease, developing an altered version of one or more key microbes, and translating this discovery into a therapy would be a long and complex undertaking that could not be accomplished without bringing together multiple areas of expertise and multiple partners. To accomplish this goal, for example, might require the following:

- DNA sequencing technology to obtain genetic information on microbes present in the body
- Life and chemical sciences experiments to further characterize the microbes detected
- Mathematical and computational tools to analyze the data generated, compare sequences, and identify potential genes associated with the disease of interest
- Public health studies to better understand the role of microbes in the particular disease state
- Engineering and synthetic biology expertise to design a microbe with altered gene expression
- Materials science knowledge to encapsulate the engineered microbe into a delivery system such as an ingestible pill
- Clinical trials and regulatory agency partnerships to approve the pill for human use
- Industry partners to scale up manufacturing and production
- Social and behavioral interventions to target the new treatment to the populations who would benefit from it

HHSN26300047, TO#47, the William R. Kenan, Jr. Institute for Engineering, Technology & Science of North Carolina State University, the Frank Hawkins Kenan Institute of Private Enterprise of the University of North Carolina at Chapel Hill, and the Connecticut Institute for Clinical and Translational Science at the University of Connecticut.

TABLE S-1 Selected Examples of Convergence Institutes that Have Been Established in the United States

- Bio-X, Stanford University
- David H. Koch Institute for Integrative Cancer Research, Massachusetts Institute of Technology
- North Campus Research Complex, University of Michigan
- Institute for Molecular Engineering, University of Chicago
- Wyss Institute for Biologically Inspired Engineering, Harvard University
- Parker H. Petit Institute for Bioengineering and Bioscience, Georgia Institute of Technology
- Janelia Farm Research Campus, Howard Hughes Medical Institute
- Lewis-Sigler Institute for Integrative Biology, Princeton University
- California Institute for Quantitative Biosciences (QB3), University of California Santa Cruz, Berkeley, and San Francisco
- Biodesign Institute, Arizona State University
- Raymond and Beverly Sackler Institute for Biological, Physical and Engineering Sciences, Yale University
- USC Michelson Center for Convergent Bioscience, University of Southern California (announced 2014)

BOX S-2
Statement of Task

The National Research Council will appoint an expert committee to explore the application of "convergence" approaches to biomedical research and beyond. This approach is intended to realize the untapped potential from the merger of multiple disciplines to address key challenges that require such close collaborations. As its primary information-gathering activity, the committee will convene a workshop to examine examples or models drawn, if possible, from a range of ongoing programs, both large and small, public and private, in which such approaches are being implemented. The goal of the workshop is to facilitate understanding of how convergence in biomedical and related research can be fostered effectively through institutional and programmatic structures and policies, education and training programs, and funding mechanisms. The resulting report will summarize the lessons learned on successful approaches to implementing convergence in different types of research institutions.

Convergence can represent a culture shift for academic organizations that are traditionally organized around discipline-based departments. Consequently, the challenges inherent in creating the necessary administrative, research, teaching, partnership, and funding structures can be significant (see Table S-2 for examples). Stakeholders across the research

TABLE S-2 Comparison of Perspectives on Common Challenges Encountered in Fostering Convergence

Common Challenge	Recommendations (NAS et al. 2004)	Perspective of this Report (2014)
Establishing effective organizational cultures, structures, and governance	Institutions should explore alternative administrative structures and business models that facilitate IDR across traditional organizational structures; institutions should develop equitable and flexible budgetary and cost-sharing policies that support IDR. Allocations of resources from high-level administration to interdisciplinary units, to further their formation and continued operation, should be considered in addition to resource allocations of discipline-driven departments and colleges.	Alternative structures must harmonize with the existing culture of investigator and laboratory autonomy. Convergent science fields provide a starting point to organize around compelling scientific and societal challenges. Factors such as differences in cost recovery models among schools of science, engineering, and medicine can complicate intra-university partnerships. Laboratories and core facilities are expensive to start up and maintain (see Sections 4.3 and 4.5).
Addressing faculty development and promotion needs	Recruitment practices, from recruitment of graduate students to hiring of faculty members, should be revised to include recruitment across department and college lines. The traditional practices and norms in hiring of faculty members and in making tenure decisions should be revised to take into account more fully the values inherent in IDR activities.	Promotion and tenure is still obtained through a primary departmental affiliation for many faculty members undertaking convergent research or associated with convergence institutes. Differences in faculty research and service expectations among science, engineering, and medical faculty may complicate collaborations, although multiple journal authors and diverse research contributors are already a norm within many science fields (see Section 4.4).

continued

TABLE S-2 Continued

Common Challenge	Recommendations (NAS et al. 2004)	Perspective of this Report (2014)
Creating education and training programs	Educators should facilitate IDR by providing educational and training opportunities for undergraduates, graduate students, and postdoctoral scholars, such as relating foundation courses, data gathering and analysis, and research activities to other fields of study and to society at large.

Institutions should support interdisciplinary education and training for students, postdoctoral scholars, researchers, and faculty by providing such mechanisms as undergraduate research opportunities, faculty team-teaching credit, and IDR management training. | Curricula at the undergraduate level need to meaningfully integrate relevant physical, mathematical, computational, and engineering concepts and examples into life science courses and vice versa in order to provide a solid foundation for undertaking convergence.

Opportunities are needed to effectively fill in gaps in training and expertise or to learn fundamentals of a new area to foster a common language and understanding. These opportunities are needed at the graduate, postdoctoral, and faculty levels (see Section 4.6). |
| Forming stakeholder partnerships | Academic institutions should develop new and strengthen existing policies and practices that lower or remove barriers to interdisciplinary research and scholarship, including developing joint programs with industry and government and nongovernment organizations.

Continuing social science, humanities, and information science–based studies of the complex social and intellectual processes that make for successful IDR are needed to deepen the understanding of these processes and to enhance the prospects for the creation and management of successful programs in specific fields and local institutions. | Establishing extramural agreements is complex and may be affected by factors such as different leadership, funding, and cost-sharing models, or different traditions and expectations around issues such as patent development and intellectual property protection.

Taking full advantage of the possibilities enabled by convergence increasingly draws upon contributions from fields such as the economic and social sciences, which have their own cultures and norms that must be considered (see Section 4.7). |

TABLE S-2 Continued

Common Challenge	Recommendations (NAS et al. 2004)	Perspective of this Report (2014)
	Funding organizations should recognize and take into consideration in their programs and processes the unique challenges faced by IDR with respect to risk, organizational mode, and time.	Government support is one component of obtaining funding for convergence. Many convergence programs have also obtained critical support from sources such as private philanthropists and foundations interested in advancing science.
Obtaining sustainable funding	Funding organizations should regularly evaluate, and if necessary redesign, their proposal and review criteria to make them appropriate for interdisciplinary activities.	Income from startup companies and venture capital investors, which may be part of convergence ecosystems, may also provide support (see Section 4.8).
	Congress should continue to encourage federal research agencies to be sensitive to maintaining a proper balance between the goal of stimulating interdisciplinary research and the need to maintain robust disciplinary research.	

NOTE: As used in the table, IDR stands for interdisciplinary research. The prior recommendations cited in the table are drawn from NAS et al. (2004, pp. 5-7).

enterprise will need to think strategically about the policies that support such efforts and how to implement and sustain them. For example, the training students receive will need to prepare them to work on challenges that cross disciplinary boundaries. The research advances enabled by convergence will ultimately need to be translated into new products and services as part of the network of partners who form the convergence ecosystem. The policies and procedures that universities use to translate technology can be better understood and improved. Because convergence relies on integrating expertise from multiple fields and multiple partners, an open and inclusive culture, a common set of concepts and metrics, and a shared set of institutional and research goals are needed to support this close collaboration. Fortunately, the toolkit to foster convergence can be informed by the base of existing literature on establishing interdisciplinary cultures, supporting team-based science, and revising science, technology, engineering, and mathematics (STEM) education and training.

It can also be informed by examples drawn from industry, which has a tradition of integrating expertise to tackle complex challenges.

The report identifies examples of strategies and practices used by institutions to facilitate convergence endeavors, such as designing educational modules, hiring faculty in transdisciplinary clusters, and establishing new research institutes. Strategies and examples drawn from the committee's data gathering include

- organizing around a common theme, problem, or scientific challenge;
- implementing management structures tailored to the challenges to convergence in each institution;
- fostering opportunities to interact formally and informally;
- changing existing faculty structures and reward systems;
- working with and across existing departments;
- embedding support for convergence in the promotion and tenure process;
- designing facilities and workspaces for convergent research;
- designing education and training programs that foster convergence;
- establishing partnership arrangements across institutions; and
- exploring sources of funding within and beyond government agencies.

No single template can be followed in establishing convergence efforts and nurturing their success. Institutions range widely in characteristics such as missions, sizes, and available budgets. The committee was nonetheless able to identify essential cultural and structural elements in successful convergence ecosystems. These elements are as follows:

People: Leadership committed to supporting convergence is key, as is the involvement of students, faculty members and staff, department chairs, and deans at multiple institutional levels. A characteristic of individual practitioners that facilitates convergence is the ability to communicate across a breadth of areas while building from strong foundations of deep expertise.

Organization: Inclusive governance systems, a goal-oriented vision, effective program management, stable support for core facilities, and flexible or catalytic funding sources are all critical to organizations seeking to build a sustainable convergence ecosystem. Organizations must also be willing to take risks and consequently accept failures or redirections as inevitable hazards at the frontiers of knowledge.

Culture: The culture needed to support convergence, as with other types of collaborative research, is one that is inclusive, supports mutual respect across disciplines, encourages opportunities to share knowledge, and fosters scientists' ability to be conversant across disciplines. Diversity of perspectives and expertise is a fundamental aspect of convergence, and interactions across such knowledge cultures may provide important lessons.

Ecosystem: The overall ecosystem of convergence involves dynamic interactions with multiple partners within and across institutions, and thus requires strategies to address the technical and logistical partnership agreements required.

The committee also identified examples of relatively simple and low cost practices that institutions could consider as first steps in fostering convergence within their organizations (Table S-3).

TABLE S-3 Ideas for Fostering Convergence with a Steady State Budget

- Encourage social events such as coffee and pizza to foster presentations and discussions of convergent research.
- Repurpose journal clubs to address convergence themes.
- Foster informal gatherings of faculty with shared interests in convergence problems and topics, which may also contribute to discussions on advancing convergent candidates for faculty positions.
- Establish mechanisms for faculty to hold joint appointments across departments and schools.
- Develop or identify online resources for convergent classes.
- Provide opportunities for experimental courses such as through online tools, collaborative teaching, and teaching "sabbaticals" to develop new courses.
- Include examples in undergraduate and introductory science classes that show how physics, chemistry, math, engineering, and biology are put into practice when dealing with current issues.
- Implement flexible course requirements for graduate students that enable them to fill gaps in knowledge needed to undertake convergent projects and/or the ability for graduate students to name and shape the area of their degree.
- Undertake cluster hires.
- Reduce bureaucratic boundaries.
- Initiate executive-in-residence programs to bring insights from practitioners in industry.
- Institute programs to encourage collaboration at a distance for faculty from different institutions and areas of science.

RECOMMENDATIONS

The 21st century will be one in which advances made in understanding the genetic and molecular basis of life are merged with contributions from the physical sciences, medicine, engineering, and beyond to achieve new revolutions at the frontiers of knowledge. Better understanding and overcoming the challenges of facilitating convergence will be an important strategy to fully realizing this goal. It is time for a systematic effort to highlight the value of convergence as a mode of research and development, and to address lingering challenges to its effective practice. This effort is needed in order to more effectively harness the potential of convergence to stimulate innovation and provide solutions to societal needs.

If the United States wishes to capture the momentum generated by convergence and foster its further development, the committee makes the following recommendations (summarized in Table S-4):

1. **Experts, funding agencies, foundations, and other partners should identify key problems whose solution requires convergence approaches in order to catalyze new research directions and guide research priorities.**

TABLE S-4 Summary of Recommendations

Actors	Actions	Desired Outcomes
National vision-setting body	• Foster coordination on convergence • Build public and professional awareness of convergence as a catalyst of new scientific and technical knowledge and applications	• Innovation and economic growth • A national infrastructure that can solve emerging problems which transcend traditional boundaries
Funder of science and technology innovation	• Identify problems that would benefit from convergence approaches • Address barriers to effective convergence, both within and across institutions	• Expanded mechanisms for funding convergent research • Collaborative proposal review across funding organizations when needed

TABLE S-4 Continued

Actors	Actions	Desired Outcomes
Academic leader	• Address barriers to effective convergence partnerships, both within and across institutions • Develop policies, practices, and guidelines to support and evaluate convergent and disciplinary research equally • Utilize the expertise of economic, social, and behavioral sciences, as well as program management and strategic planning fields when planning an initiative	• Recruitment practices, cost-recovery models, and research support policies that facilitate convergence, including catalytic seed funding • Promotion and tenure policies that recognize the importance of convergence and have unique evaluation criteria for those faculty • Evidence-based practices for facilitating convergence effectively • More convergence efforts, partnerships, synergies, and collaborations, particularly at small universities and institutions that serve traditionally underrepresented groups
Government laboratory	• Develop partnerships, synergies and collaborations with colleagues across institutions • Facilitate efficient transfer of technologies derived from convergence research	• Evidence-based practices for facilitating convergence effectively • New products and services derived from convergent research
Industry, medical, or regulatory stakeholder	• Address barriers to effective convergence partnerships across institutions • Facilitate efficient transfer of technologies derived from convergence research	• Expanded mechanisms for funding convergent research • New products and services derived from convergent research

2. Research institutions, funding agencies, foundations, and other partners should address barriers to effective convergence as they arise, including expanding mechanisms for funding convergence efforts and supporting collaborative proposal review across funding partners. Institutional programs such as seed funding to catalyze collaborations should be implemented or expanded.

3. Institutions should review their administrative structures, faculty recruitment and promotion practices, cost recovery models, and research support policies to identify and reduce roadblocks to the formation of inter- and intrainstitutional partnerships that facilitate convergence.

4. Academic institutions should develop hiring and promotion policies that include explicit guidelines to recognize the importance of both convergent and disciplinary scholarship, and include criteria to fairly evaluate them.

5. Those interested in fostering convergence should identify evidence-based practices that have facilitated convergence by drawing on the expertise of economic, social, and behavioral sciences, as well as program management and strategic planning. Understanding the barriers and strategies to practicing convergence would improve practical guidance on how institutions can structure and sustain a convergence program.

6. Leaders and practitioners who have fostered a convergence culture in their organizations and laboratories should develop partnerships, synergies, and collaborations with their colleagues in other organizations—especially in small universities and institutions that serve traditionally underrepresented groups—to help these partnering institutions establish and nurture convergence efforts while furthering the interests of their own.

7. Best practices on the effective transfer of technologies from research organizations into the private sector should be collected, established, and disseminated. For convergent approaches to enable innovation and stimulate future economic development, research advances need to be translated into new products and services.

In order to most effectively achieve these goals, coordination is required to move beyond the patchwork of current efforts. The outcome-focused, boundary-crossing approach embodied by the process of convergence has been gaining momentum. Institutions and science practitioners are aware of the increasing push to link basic research to broader goals, even if potential applications of fundamental research are in the uncertain future. Many research questions now require combinations of expertise to solve. University commercialization activities such as patent applications continue to increase. Nevertheless, fostering the process of convergence successfully remains a challenge. As a result, the committee makes a final recommendation:

8. **National coordination on convergence is needed to support the infrastructure to solve emerging problems that transcend traditional boundaries. Stakeholders across the ecosystem of convergence—including agencies, foundations, academic and industry leaders, clinicians, and scientific practitioners—should collaborate to build awareness of the role of convergence in advancing science and technology and stimulating innovation for the benefit of society.**

NATIONAL COORDINATION IS NEEDED

A national focus on convergence would accomplish several goals. It would catalyze stakeholders to identify emerging topics at the frontiers of science where convergence will be critical to achieving new insights and would engage the vibrant community of institutional leaders and interested researchers, both younger and senior, who are already undertaking convergence. Community input on the investment priorities in research, education, and infrastructure will help maximize the benefits of convergence to society. Examples such as the visioning activities undertaken by the Computing Community Consortium and researcher participation in the conception of the Brain Research through Advancing Innovative Neurotechnologies (BRAIN) initiative[3] could provide useful models.

Detailed study on the barriers and strategies to practicing conver-

---

[3] The Computing Community Consortium, which operates through the Computing Research Association, identifies research opportunities and directions for the field (see http://www.cra.org/ccc/). The BRAIN initiative, announced by President Obama in 2013 and initially supported by the National Institutes of Health, National Science Foundation, Defense Advanced Research Projects Agency, Howard Hughes Medical Institute, Kavli Foundation, Allen Institute for Brain Science, and Salk Institute for Biological Studies is a grand challenge effort to improve understanding of dynamic brain processes. Further information is available at http://www.whitehouse.gov/share/brain-initiative.

gence would improve practical guidance on how to structure a convergence program at an institution and what policies and agreements are necessary to sustain one. Established convergence institutes of a variety of ages (i.e., those established in the 1990s to those just now being created) provide a set of case studies for future programs. The histories and practices of those institutes can, in principle, be exploited to understand how to overcome barriers to convergence, how to nurture and sustain convergence, and how to evaluate success of convergence efforts. Yet, the information the committee was able to gather was still largely anecdotal in nature, based on single case studies and/or short time periods. The community interested in fostering convergence needs mechanisms to share lessons learned more widely and to translate those practices across diverse institutional settings.

The social sciences and humanities are undertapped resources for convergence efforts. An enhanced and expanded partnership among convergence practitioners from multiple fields in the life, physical, and engineering sciences, the economic, social, and behavioral science and humanities research communities, and institutional leaders could be invaluable. The role of the economic, social, and behavioral sciences and humanities in convergence is multifaceted. Areas of convergent research, such as cognitive neuroscience, already benefit from the integration of behavioral, biological, and medical sciences. Moreover, many of the obstacles to effective convergence involve interpersonal interactions, and the translation of advances enabled by convergence into societal benefits involves economic, social, and behavioral dimensions. A focus on convergence would draw attention to resources available in areas such as the study of interdisciplinary and transdisciplinary success, the process of team science, and the evaluation of collaborative research. It would enable convergence practitioners, funders, and users to apply these research contributions toward catalyzing convergence in a variety of settings.

Within the academic community, convergence efforts could and should draw in a greater number of participants from institutions beyond the large, research-intensive university systems that predominated in the committee's data-gathering, along with partners such as national laboratories, clinics, and industry. Coordination on fostering convergence would stimulate the engagement of core partners in the ecosystem of convergence from discovery to application and would also provide opportunities for multinational partnerships with centers that have been established elsewhere in the world. Diversity of viewpoints and experiences enables innovation, and the convergence approach provides an opportunity to increase diversity and harness it for the benefit of all societies.

Finally, convergence efforts cross boundaries of life, health, physical, and engineering sciences and thus also cross boundaries among funding agencies that support biomedical research, such as the National Institutes of Health (NIH), and those that have traditionally supported research in the physical sciences, such as the Department of Energy (DOE), National Science Foundation (NSF), and Department of Defense (DOD). National coordination on convergence would provide a platform for funding agencies and foundations to discuss emerging opportunities for collaboration, learn about programs and practices being implemented at other agencies, and serve as a network of resources for each other. The power of such cross-agency efforts at the interface between life and physical sciences is exemplified by the success of the Human Genome Initiative, which was supported collaboratively by NIH and DOE.

National coordination would provide a multiagency and multistakeholder framework of shared goals; leverage the interests and strengths of research and development agencies such as NIH, NSF, DOE, and DOD and regulatory agencies such as the U.S. Department of Agriculture and the Food and Drug Administration; foster networks of convergence centers and practitioners in academic, industrial, and clinical settings; and engage the imagination of future scientists and innovators. Convergence, which brings together knowledge and tools from life sciences, physical sciences, medicine, engineering, and beyond to stimulate innovative research and address compelling technical and societal challenges, has a scope that is diverse and multisectorial. Institutions, funding agencies, and foundations have made positive strides in establishing centers of convergence and identifying practices that nurture convergence ecosystems. Nevertheless, practical challenges remain. An emphasis on coordination would enable the United States to better harness the power of convergence to yield new knowledge and stimulate transformative innovation.

Introduction

Convergence is an approach to problem solving that integrates expertise from life sciences with physical, mathematical, and computational sciences,[1] medicine, and engineering to form comprehensive synthetic frameworks that merge areas of knowledge from multiple fields to address specific challenges. Convergence builds on fundamental progress made within individual disciplines but represents a way of thinking about the process of research and the types of strategies that enable it as emerging scientific and societal challenges cut across disciplinary boundaries in these fields. The concept of convergence as represented in this report is thus meant to capture two dimensions: the convergence of the subsets of expertise necessary to address a set of research problems, and the formation of the web of partnerships involved in supporting such scientific investigations and enabling the resulting advances to be translated into new forms of innovation and new products.

Convergence represents a cultural shift for academic organizations that have been traditionally organized around discipline-based departments. The overall ecosystem needed to foster and sustain convergence draws not only on academic contributors but increasingly also on the cross-fertilization of ideas with stakeholders and partners from national laboratories, industry, clinical settings, and funding bodies, as well as

---

[1] Throughout the rest of the report, the term "physical sciences" is commonly used as shorthand to include fields such as physics, chemistry, materials science, and the mathematical and computational sciences.

insights from economic, social, and behavioral sciences. The process of convergence is applicable to basic science discovery as well as translational application. Because it is commonly focused on achieving an outcome to a challenge at the frontiers of knowledge, many convergence efforts include an entrepreneurship component that leads to the development of a surrounding web of startup companies and economic innovation.

1.1 A SCIENCE AND TECHNOLOGY REVOLUTION IS OCCURRING

During the 20th century, major breakthroughs in advancing research-based knowledge and its applications to societal problems resulted from bringing together disciplines across physical sciences and engineering. Satellite-based global positioning systems that applied physical principles, including the development of accurate atomic clocks corrected for gravitational and atmospheric effects, now underpin vehicle navigation systems and provide location data for ubiquitous mobile phone and tablet computer apps (IOP 2009; Lucibella 2012). The combination of an image sensor such as a charge-coupled device that converts light into electrical signals, signal processing into images that can be stored and printed, and the ability to handle millions of pixels of data fueled the adoption of digital cameras, which were first marketed as consumer products in the late 1980s and early 1990s. The field of nanotechnology was built on the development of analytical technologies such as the scanning tunneling microscope as well as materials science and surface chemistry that enabled scientists to understand and control properties at the atomic scale. Today nanomaterials are found in products ranging from conductive inks for printed electronics to advanced batteries (NNI 2014). In each case integrating methods and tools from physical sciences and engineering were keys to both new knowledge and product innovation.

It has been postulated that the 21st century will become the "century of biology," enabled by the impressive progress made in understanding the molecular basis of life and in applying that knowledge in new directions (Venter and Cohen 2004; Dyson 2007). Determination of the structure of DNA in 1953 led to the elucidation of the central dogma of biology and the development of principles relating DNA's structure to the mechanisms of reproduction and translation, providing for the first time a unifying concept of how information was transmitted within the cell and between generations. Within 20 years, the scientific community had developed the ability to not only sequence and synthesize a gene but to combine genes and pieces of genes, founding the age of biotechnology. Fifty years on, the technology to sequence, computationally compare, and interact with the complexity of the human genome, and to do all of that at relatively low cost, in turn spawned revolutions in areas ranging from genomics to bioinformatics. A critical dimension of this new century will be the further integration of life sciences into physical sciences and engineering fields, and vice versa. Making use of the wealth of information that molecular biology, genomics, and the other "omics" fields are now yielding will require contributions from multiple disciplines, moving beyond the first revolution of interdisciplinary molecular and cellular biology and the second revolution of genomics to a third revolution marked by transformative integration of life sciences, physical sciences, medicine, and engineering (Sharp and Langer 2011; Sharp et al. 2011) (see Figure 1-1).

The process of this convergence among life and health sciences, physical sciences, and engineering along with the increasing incorporation of contributions from social and economic sciences has the potential to fundamentally impact the organization and conduct of research in the com-

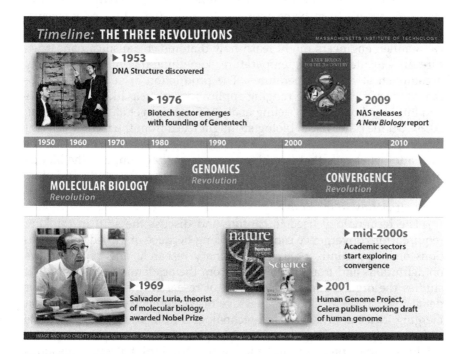

FIGURE 1-1 The continuing integration of life sciences, physical sciences, medicine, and engineering represents a third revolution in life sciences, building on prior revolutions in molecular biology and genomics.
SOURCE: Courtesy of Phillip A. Sharp, Institute Professor, Massachusetts Institute of Technology.

ing decades. Exploring why this process represents a promising frontier of new knowledge and what strategies can nurture it within institutional structures will constitute both an opportunity and an ongoing challenge for organizations across the research enterprise.

1.2 CONVERGENCE IS AN EXPANDED FORM OF INTERDISCIPLINARY RESEARCH

The goal of merging expertise to address complex problems is not new, and there are myriad examples in which researchers from multiple disciplines have worked together to solve problems that are beyond the scope of individual scientific areas. Most often described as an "interdisciplinary" approach, this goal has been a common feature of industrial research laboratories since the 1920s, and many research initiatives based in academic laboratories also rely on collaboration among investigators from more than one field. At the heart of the current momentum for convergence, however, is the realization that physical and biological sciences can each benefit from being more fully integrated into the intellectual milieu of the other. By working together in a coordinated and reciprocal manner, engineers might learn how diatoms create silica nanostructures in seawater at room temperature, something that humans can only accomplish at high temperatures. The production of such silica nanostructures may have wide-ranging applications in areas like novel sensors and improved batteries (Vrieling et al. 2005; Khripin et al. 2011; Luo et al. 2013). On the other hand, biologists might learn from the techniques that nanoengineers are developing for surmounting physical barriers, such as the endothelial cells that line blood vessels or that comprise the blood–brain barrier (Chrastina et al. 2011; Jain 2012; Patel et al. 2013; Tosi et al. 2013). This knowledge could lead to new targeted therapeutics delivered more efficiently in the body.

The terminology used to capture and discuss the shift in thinking required for convergence can be confusing because of varied interpretations of inter-, multi-, or transdisciplinary research. This report draws on definitions and framing concepts from the academic community that studies the organization and conduct of research (discussed in greater detail in Chapter 3). The key message of convergence, however, is that merging ideas, approaches, and technologies from widely diverse fields of knowledge at a high level of integration is one crucial strategy for solving complex problems and addressing complex intellectual questions underlying emerging disciplines. Of necessity, convergence requires an open and inclusive culture, and requires practitioners to move beyond a single language to being conversant across disciplines and to building a common set of concepts and metrics and a common understanding about goals.

In this way, convergence represents an expanded form of interdisciplinarity in which bodies of specialized knowledge comprise "macro" domains of research activity that together create a unified whole. When integrated effectively, these convergent macro domains offer the possibility of a new paradigm capable of generating ideas, discoveries, methodological and conceptual approaches, and tools that stimulate advances in basic research and lead to new inventions, innovations, treatment protocols, and forms and strategies of education and training. Such a comprehensive level of integration, without specifically using the term "convergence," has been conceptualized in several recent reports (Figure 1-2).

When done well, convergence can represent a roadmap for innovation, and in particular for generating what has been called combinatorial innovation, a process that happens when a new technology or set of technologies offers a rich set of components that can be combined and recombined to create new products and services. These components catalyze a technology boom as innovators from multiple fields work through the possibilities.

In biomedicine, convergence will be one essential strategy for making progress in the treatment of disease to improve health outcomes while lowering costs, but a number of real-world problems do not respect disciplinary boundaries and a convergence approach has the potential to benefit many areas of research and development. Examples of such problems include meeting the world's need for secure food supplies on a hotter, drier planet while reducing the environmental footprint of agriculture; providing new treatments for the chronic illnesses that are plaguing an increasing number of people worldwide; and directly attacking the mechanisms of aging in ways beyond addressing the individual diseases of aging. Chapter 2 highlights further examples of convergence in action.

1.3 CONVERGENT THINKING IS ADVANCING SCIENCE

Numerous reports over the past decade have explored the advances enabled when disciplines come together in integrated partnerships. Several address broad questions of how integrative and collaborative research can be fostered and what this means for the future of the American research enterprise. Others focus on specific research challenges at the intersection of the physical and life sciences or present a vision for the future of biology.

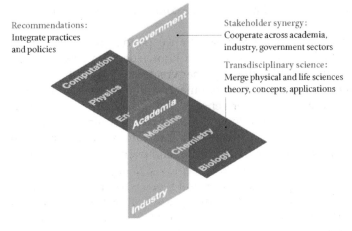

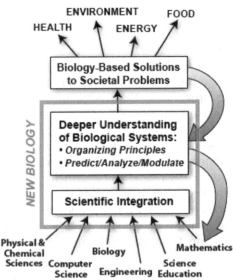

FIGURE 1-2 Two representations of the process of integration represented by convergence. Top, in order to take advantage of new opportunities, a merger of expertise from life and physical sciences and synergy across academic, industry, and government sectors is needed. Bottom, the New Biology, which focuses on the life sciences, draws on integration of multiple scientific fields in the creation of biology-based solutions to societal challenges.

SOURCE: Top, reprinted by permission of the American Academy of Arts and Sciences; (The figure is found in the Executive Summary of ARISE II, Advancing Research in Science and Engineering: Unleashing America's Research & Innovation Enterprise, available at http://www.amacad.org/multimedia/pdfs/ARISEII_ExecutiveSummary.pdf). Bottom, NRC 2009, p. 18.

1.3.1 The Research Ecosystem Involves Multiple
Disciplines and Multiple Partners

A recent report from the American Academy of Arts and Sciences makes the case that research is at a tipping point in a transition from ultra-specialization and defined problems to one in which integrative and collaborative approaches are needed to solve complex challenges. The report examines how research practices and policies will need to be revised in order to integrate over two planes necessary to address this pivotal point: across disciplines in the form of transdisciplinary and convergent science, and across stakeholders to produce additional synergy and account for the changing funding landscape (see Figure 1-2, top). The report argues that, without both of these planes, the process represented by convergence cannot effectively happen (American Academy of Arts and Sciences 2013).

The report also emphasizes a need for cooperative, synergistic interactions among the academic, government, and private sectors throughout the discovery and development process. One of the report's conclusions is that historical differences exist in the culture of physical sciences and engineering, on the one hand, and life sciences and medicine, on the other. While engineering and the physical sciences have a rich tradition of placing discovery and application on a continuum, the ends of this spectrum have traditionally been disconnected in the life sciences and medicine. For example, the report notes that most of the company spinoffs generated by the genomics revolution have been initiated by physical scientists and chemical engineers. As a result, the report argues that it will be imperative for many biologists to develop a fuller awareness and capacity for applications of research.

Similarly, a recent report from the National Research Council discusses the roles of research universities as assets for the future and recommends actions to maintain and further strengthen them for the benefit of U.S. science and technology (NRC 2012a). The report's vision emphasizes many of the characteristics highlighted by the American Academy of Arts and Sciences, including a need for comprehensive partnerships among government, academia, and industry to "facilitate the transfer of knowledge, ideas, and technology to society and accelerate 'time to innovation' in order to achieve our national goals" (NRC 2012a, p. 11).

1.3.2 Convergence Will Accelerate Discovery and Innovation

An array of reports from the National Research Council (NRC) have examined key opportunities enabled by science that occur at the intersections of disciplines and have set forth the view that multiple fields are poised to make significant advances if communities collaborate across life, physical, mathematical, computational, and engineering fields. These publications include *Mathematics and 21st Century Biology* (NRC 2005a), *Catalyzing Inquiry at the Interface of Computing and Biology* (NRC 2005b), *Inspired by Biology: From Molecules to Materials to Machines* (NRC 2008), *A New Biology for the 21st Century* (NRC 2009), *Research at the Intersection of the Physical and Life Sciences* (NRC 2010), and *Research Frontiers in Bioinspired Energy: Molecular-Level Learning from Natural Systems: A Workshop* (NRC 2012b). Such reports, along with others from outside the NRC, provide compelling examples of what can be achieved by drawing together diverse areas of expertise and argue that activities conducted at the interface between life and physical sciences will continue to be an integral part of the scientific enterprise looking toward the future. *A New Biology*, in particular, argues that advances in biological research will accelerate if directed toward grand challenges and that integrating life sciences research with other disciplines will gain a deeper understanding of biological systems and achieve new biology-based solutions to critical societal problems in the areas of health, environment, energy, and food (see Figure 1-2, bottom).

Many of these earlier reports did not specifically adopt the terminology of "convergence" to refer to the goal of merging expertise across disciplines, although the concept they described is similar in intent. A specific vision for the convergence of life sciences, physical sciences, medicine, and engineering to advance health was more fully articulated by scientists and leaders at the Massachusetts Institute of Technology (Sharp and Langer 2011; Sharp et al. 2011). It has continued to capture the attention of scientists who practice at these convergent interfaces (Sharp and Langer 2013; Sharp and Leshner 2014).

1.3.3 Convergence Is About Science and Society

A recent report expands this concept of convergence to encompass the broad convergence of knowledge, technology, and society across multiple dimensions (Roco et al. 2013). Convergence is placed in the context of a creative "convergence–divergence" process that brings areas of knowledge together into a new system to spin off applications and elements that can in turn be recombined and integrated. Research activities from across a spectrum including pure basic research, use-inspired basic research, and "vision-inspired" basic research, as well as applied research, are needed throughout this repeating cycle (Figure 1-3). Although placing convergence in a very broad context, the report emphasizes a critical role of the merging of life and physical sciences expertise. In their chapter *Implications: Human Health and Physical Potential*, for example, Urban and Grodzinski state, "over the next ten years, the major scientific infrastruc-

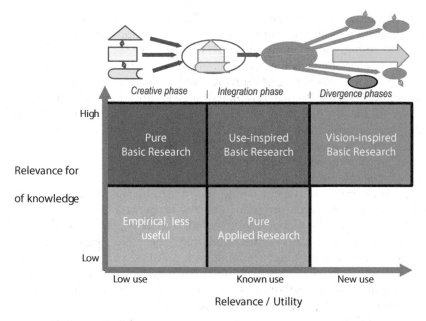

FIGURE 1-3 The role of research in the convergence–divergence process. Scientific research can be characterized by its motivation to advance fundamental knowledge and have practical utility. Roco et al. add a new box for "vision-inspired basic research" that explores transformative ideas beyond known applications. These transformative basic science components become pieces that can be recombined to generate convergent advances.
SOURCE: Courtesy of M. C. Roco, adapted from Figure 4.5 in Roco et al. 2013.

ture needed will be an effort to define these 'laws of biology' within a convergence approach that nurtures engagement of the physics and physical sciences research communities" (Urban and Grodzinski 2013, p. 184).

1.3.4 Implementing Convergence Builds on Prior Reports

In order to be successful at harnessing the combined transformative potential of life and physical sciences with engineering, key stakeholders across the research enterprise need to think strategically about the policies necessary to support such efforts and how to implement and sustain them. The challenges inherent in creating new research, teaching, institutional, funding, partnership, and other structures likely to be required as part of successful convergence efforts can be enormous. The report *Facilitating Interdisciplinary Research*, published by the National Research

Council almost a decade ago (NAS et al. 2004), lays a foundation for how collaborative scientific endeavors can be fostered and provides numerous recommendations, many of which can be extended for the purpose of convergence. In fact, the top three actions identified by 341 survey respondents in 2004 for institutions seeking to support interdisciplinary research (IDR) were "to foster a collaborative environment (26.5 percent), to provide faculty incentives (including hiring and tenure policies) that reflect and reward involvement in IDR (18.4 percent), and to provide seed money for IDR projects (11.1 percent)" (NAS et al. 2004, p. 270). These points continue to be strongly echoed in the committee's data gathering for the present report.

Despite progress in establishing interdisciplinary, transdisciplinary, and convergent research programs and the existence of agency policies designed to support collaborative scientific endeavors, challenges clearly remain. The Roco et al. volume notes that "there has been a growing appreciation in scientific and academic communities worldwide that converging technologies . . . are likely to create important advances toward societal gain," but the authors continue to raise the concern that "the R&D focus for converging technologies publications has remained reactive (or 'coincidental') to various opportunities for collaboration rather than being driven by a holistic, systematic, proactive approach towards promoting convergence" (Roco et al. 2013, p. 138). Organizations and practitioners wishing to undertake convergence face a lack of practical guidance in how to do it.

The present report does not seek to re-tread all of the ground covered by these prior activities. Rather, it revisits key themes they highlighted and provides tailored examples of strategies relevant to addressing the continuing challenges of fostering convergence among life sciences, physical sciences, medicine, and engineering in different settings. It also considers the opportunities and challenges that arise from expanding convergent research initiatives to include contributions from additional fields such as the economic and social sciences and humanities.

1.4 INSTITUTIONS NEED GUIDANCE TO FOSTER CONVERGENCE EFFECTIVELY

Now is an opportune time to consider steps that can be taken to foster convergence among biological, physical, and engineering sciences. Institutions continue to face a lack of guidance on how to establish effective programs, what challenges they are likely to encounter, and what strategies other organizations have used to solve the issues that arise. The present study was undertaken to help address this gap and to provide an opportunity for members of the research community to come together and discuss their challenges. Responding to the messages from reports such as those above and the needs of their scientists and communities, institutions have increasingly moved to implement programs that foster convergence or are interested in how they can better facilitate convergent research. The number of research universities that are making investments in convergence is increasing and so, too, is the diversity of institutional practices being used to facilitate convergence, ranging from new educational modules (see Section 4.6), to cluster hiring (Section 4.4), to establishing multidisciplinary research institutes (Section 4.3). The success of the National Academies Keck Futures Initiative at catalyzing the formation of research teams that start new avenues of investigation is yet another example of the growing appreciation of the role of convergence among many in both the research and policy worlds (Porter et al. 2008; NAS et al. 2013).

In parallel, the federal government has announced funding for several large convergent initiatives focused around specific research areas. The Brain Research through Advancing Innovative Neurotechnologies (BRAIN) initiative is a multiagency effort led by the National Institutes of Health (NIH), Defense Advanced Research Projects Agency (DARPA), and the National Science Foundation (NSF) with significant support from private research institutions and foundations. It seeks to generate new understanding about how the brain works and, to succeed, it will require convergence among fields such as neuroscience, nanoscience, synthetic biology, genetics, optics, computer science, and informatics. The Tissue Chip Project, a collaboration among NIH, DARPA, and the Food and Drug Administration, aims to foster convergence among tissue engineering, cell biology, microfluidics, analytical chemistry, physiology, drug development, and regulatory science to develop three-dimensional chips that mimic human physiology. NSF's Integrated Support Promoting Interdisciplinary Research and Education program, the National Cancer Institute's Alliance for Cancer Nanotechnology and Physical Sciences Oncology Centers, and DARPA's Quantitative Effects in Biological Environments are other examples.

Despite strong models, however, a number of cultural and institutional roadblocks slow implementation of convergence and creation of a self-sustaining ecosystem of convergence. The committee's task was to explore the mechanisms used by organizations and programs to support convergent research and to distill messages that arose into a report that seeks to provide informed guidance for the community (see Box 1-1 for the full statement of task and Appendix A for committee member biographies).

A primary mechanism by which the committee gathered information on relevant programs and activities was its workshop on "Key Challenges

BOX 1-1
Statement of Task

The National Research Council will appoint an expert committee to explore the application of "convergence" approaches to biomedical research and beyond. This approach is intended to realize the untapped potential from the merger of multiple disciplines to address key challenges that require such close collaborations. As its primary information-gathering activity, the committee will convene a workshop to examine examples or models drawn, if possible, from a range of ongoing programs, both large and small, public and private, in which such approaches are being implemented. The goal of the workshop is to facilitate understanding of how convergence in biomedical and related research can be fostered effectively through institutional and programmatic structures and policies, education and training programs, and funding mechanisms. The resulting report will summarize the lessons learned on successful approaches to implementing convergence in different types of research institutions.

in the Implementation of Convergence," held September 16-17, 2013. A cross section of over 100 participants ranging from graduate students to senior institutional leaders to scientists from foundations and agencies gathered at the National Academy of Sciences in Washington, D.C. (see Appendix B). The group discussed examples of programs that had been created and what has worked and not worked in varied settings, with an emphasis on strategies to tackle practical needs and challenges in areas such as organizational infrastructure, faculty development, education and training, and the formation of interinstitutional partnerships. The result of the workshop discussions and additional research undertaken by the committee is the following report, which seeks to harness the promise of the concept of convergence and channel it into the policies, structures, and networks that will better enable it to realize its goals.

1.5 ORGANIZATION OF THE REPORT

The report explores convergence in context and in action—examining why it is a paradigm for generating innovative science, why and how institutions and agencies can foster cultures of convergence, and why further coordination among the academic, clinical, industrial, and funding communities interested in convergence is needed. Chapter 2 provides examples of convergence in action that demonstrate the promise of convergent thinking in advancing knowledge and in achieving problem-based solutions at the interfaces of life, medical, physical, and engineering sciences, and beyond. The chapter also highlights some of the ways that a convergence ecosystem cross-fertilizes interactions with industry partners to help stimulate biotechnology innovation. Chapter 3 presents a snapshot of research in some of the foundational areas that inform an understanding of convergence, especially transdisciplinarity and team science and new approaches in science, technology, engineering, and mathematics education. The report does not attempt to provide an authoritative review of these rich and diverse fields. Rather, it seeks to make science practitioners and institutional leaders aware of complementary bodies of knowledge that may provide further insights into ways they can meet the challenge of nurturing environments in which convergence occurs. Chapter 4 builds on the examples presented during the project's data-gathering workshop as it begins to formulate a picture of how convergence can be fostered in organizational settings. Finally, Chapter 5 provides the committee's overall conclusions and recommendations.

Convergence in Action

Before turning to the more detailed discussion of institutional frameworks for fostering convergence, this chapter discusses five examples that illustrate why convergence is a fruitful concept and demonstrate its power to yield scientific insights applied to real-world problems.

2.1 A KNOWLEDGE NETWORK WILL IMPROVE DISEASE TREATMENT

"One of the most exciting illustrations of the possibilities of convergence is in the area of precision medicine. By precision medicine I mean the notion of treatments, diagnostics, approaches to the patient that are increasingly focused on the individual specific needs of that particular patient" (Harvey Fineberg, Workshop on Key Challenges in the Implementation of Convergence, September 16-17, 2013, Washington, DC). Recent advances in biomedical research have created an explosion of data that could be used to develop this concept of precision medicine—a more precise and more accurate classification of disease that could revolutionize diagnosis, therapy, and clinical decisions, leading to more individualized treatments and improved outcomes for patients. For example, as the cost of sequencing genomes continues to fall, the increase in the amount of available genetic data is boosting understanding of the root causes of specific diseases and conditions, such as high cholesterol. Using genomic data, scientists have already found that a significant number of patients with high cholesterol have a nonfunctional copy of a gene that encodes a low-density lipoprotein receptor. For these individuals, lifestyle interventions such as diet and exercise alone are ineffective at reducing the early onset of cardiovascular disease. Identifying these patients would allow their doctors to prescribe statin drugs at an early age, rather than first attempting to control cholesterol with diet and exercise.

However, it can take years for advances in biomedical research to reach doctors and patients, and in the meantime health care expenditures are incurred for treatments that are only effective in specific subgroups. Although the increasing use of electronic patient records is making it easier for healthcare providers to record clinical data, researchers frequently do not have access to this base of information. In order to find groups of patients for study, researchers often use informal referral networks to identify physicians working with patients with diseases of interest. Regulations that govern patient privacy, such as the Health Insurance Portability and Accountability Act (HIPAA) also create obstacles to linking genomic and clinical data.

Convergence among the biomedical, technological, clinical, and regulatory fields could help create a knowledge network for precision medicine that integrates these multiple sources of information (Figure 2-1). Molecular data, medical histories, information on social and physical environments, and health outcomes could be continuously updated and made accessible to the research community, health care providers, and the public. Analyzing connections between information sets—for example, information on patients' genomes and environmental exposures—would help scientists to formulate and test disease mechanisms and clinicians to develop new treatments based on unique features of a disease and tailored to each patient.

The knowledge network created by this vision is a tool. One example of the type of impact it might eventually enable would be to improve treatment and enhance disease survival rates among multiple demographic and socioeconomic groups, an outcome that would require life, medical, behavioral, social, and systems science contributions. The recognition of social factors in contributing to health disparities, increasing compliance with medical recommendations, and improving the organization and delivery of health care provides an additional opportunity to engage the expertise of many fields (Pescosolido et al. 2012).

2.2 THREE DIMENSIONAL PRINTING WILL BRING NEW HEALTHCARE OPTIONS

After years of debilitating pain caused by arthritis, patient Brook Hayes was in urgent need of a hip replacement. But her orthopedic

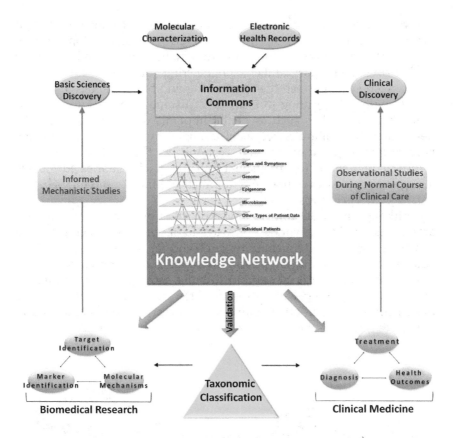

FIGURE 2-1 Building a biomedical knowledge network for basic discovery and medicine. At the center of a comprehensive biomedical information network is an information commons that contains disease information linked to individual patients and is continuously updated by a wide set of new data emerging though observational studies during the course of normal health care.
SOURCE: NRC 2011a, p. 52.

surgeon explained that Brook's small stature and severe hip deformities meant that standard hip replacement surgery would not work. She needed customized hip implants—and to build them, her medical team turned to three-dimensional (3D) printing technology (Mayo Clinic 2013). Used industrially for the past several decades, 3D printers work by following instructions from a computer to deposit thin layers of material into structures. Because there is no human operator or hard-coded machine instructions, and no molds to design or special tools needed, 3D printers can build a wide variety of objects from scratch in hours. The technology allows engineers to experiment with new ideas and numerous design iterations quickly and cheaply, and is often used to develop intricate parts used in architecture, industrial design, automotive and aerospace engineering, the military, and civil engineering (Gross et al. 2014).

Convergence between the engineering and biotechnology worlds is now bringing 3D printing to medicine. Customized joint implants and other medical devices such as dental implants or hearing aids can be designed using computerized axial tomography scans of the patient's body and constructed on demand. Not only are the finished devices the right size and shape for the patient, but the quickly fabricated models also give surgeons an opportunity to practice difficult procedures before entering the operating theater.

Although most 3D printers make objects from plastics, researchers around the world are working on ways to 3D print with living cells to construct organs and tissues for research and for use in transplantation. Unlike traditional tissue engineering techniques, which involve seeding living cells on an artificial scaffold to build cartilage, bone, or muscle, biological 3D printing will, in theory, allow researchers to control the placement of cells and other components to more closely mimic natural structures (Figure 2-2) (Fountain 2013; Ozbolat and Yu 2013).

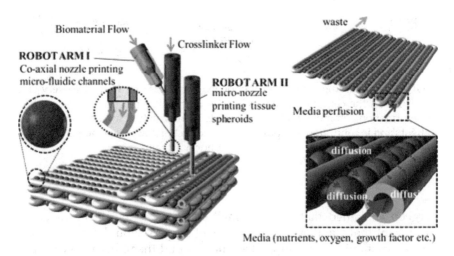

FIGURE 2-2 Conceptual model of three dimensional printing for organs and tissues. Droplets of cells and biomaterials are deposited layer by layer in 3D assemblies. A separate nozzle creates microfluidic channels that can circulate perfusion media.
SOURCE: Copyright 2013 IEEE. Reprinted, with permission, from Ozbolat and Yu 2013, Fig. 5.

Applying 3D printing to biomedical uses requires integrating knowl-edge from life sciences on how to sustain the viability of cells throughout the printing process, from material science on biocompatible scaffolding to support the cells, and from electrical and mechanical engineering to design and construct the device. Addressing this research frontier by bringing together multiple fields has led to progress that no single disci-pline could have achieved alone.

Printing a complex, functional organ such as a heart or liver for patient transplantation is still beyond reach, but academic and industrial research communities have made progress toward this goal, for example, by constructing strips of liver cells that can be used to test experimental drugs. Other laboratories have experimented with 3D printing of skin or heart cells that might be used for skin grafts or to repair damage from heart attacks (Chang et al. 2011; Guillotin and Guillemot 2011; Ferris et al. 2013; Koch et al. 2013; Organovo 2014). Further contributions will be needed for novel 3D products, such as printed bones, tissues, and organs, to move through the necessary regulatory channels to be approved for widespread use in clinical settings.

2.3 CONVERGENCE OCCURS IN FEDERAL AGENCIES: ARPA-E

Convergence occurs not only in academic settings, but is also embed-ded in innovative government programs. The Department of Energy's Advanced Research Projects Agency–Energy (ARPA–E) was authorized under the 2007 America COMPETES Act and established in 2009 with a goal of "translat[ing] science into quantum leaps in energy technologies" (Majumdar 2013). The program has had several successful convergent research efforts during its short history. One such project aimed to bridge the fields of synthetic biology, microbiology, and chemistry to develop electrofuels—a new, potentially more efficient type of renewable fuel (Ritter 2011; ARPA–E 2014).

Currently, most biofuels are produced from plants, which harvest the sun's energy and convert it into chemical energy via photosynthesis. However, photosynthesis is an inefficient energy-conversion process, and growing sufficient plant material requires large areas of farmland and inputs of resources such as water and fertilizer. In contrast, electrofuels are produced by microorganisms that are able to get energy directly from electricity or from chemicals such as hydrogen or ammonia. The biore-actors that house the microorganisms do not require large amounts of agricultural land and have the potential to be produced more efficiently.

The idea of developing the ARPA–E electrofuels program came out of a 2-day workshop and met with skepticism when it was first proposed (Majumdar 2013). However, within 18 months, the effort had succeeded in bringing together expertise from partners within industry and academia to create an electrofuel using hydrogen and carbon dioxide as input resources. For example, OPX Biotechnologies, a Colorado-based renewable chemicals company, used microbial extremophiles to produce energy rich, long chain fatty acid molecules for a variety of industrial applications. Meanwhile, synthetic biologists at North Carolina State University developed chemical processes to convert fatty acids into liquid fuels. To create the new electrofuel, researchers isolated a bacterium with the natural ability to use hydrogen and carbon dioxide for growth and used a proprietary technique called EDGE (efficiency-directed genome engineering) to modify the microorganism to divert energy and carbon away from growth and toward the production of fatty acids—making it more efficient for fuel production. Synthetic biologists next used a series of chemical processes to convert the fatty acid precursors into liquid transportation fuels. The project exemplifies how an approach that drew on the complementary expertise of several groups of researchers could optimize electrofuel production.

2.4 CONVERGENCE OCCURS IN INDUSTRY: BIOTECHNOLOGY

Industry often has a naturally interdisciplinary outlook to problem-solving approaches, and is an ally and partner in many convergence efforts.[1] The history of convergence in commercial biotechnology provides a view of how organizational cultures that support research and innovation have developed in the past in these settings. The example of the founding of Illumina (see Box 2-1) may also provide insights on the process of fostering convergence that are applicable for institutions beyond the commercial sector.

Commercial innovators both catalyze and deliver the social benefits of research convergence. Their position in the biomedical enterprise often enables them to engage the challenges and embrace the opportunities of convergence. The institutional flexibility of commercial enterprises can lower hurdles to convergence because a dynamic commercial sector ignores boundaries between domains of knowledge and removes barriers in pursuit of new opportunities. Moreover, commercial organizations are active at the interface of convergent research and the broader social context that can accelerate or hinder new developments. The participation of those with expertise in nontechnical areas including finance, economics,

---

[1]Mention of specific companies in the report is made for illustrative purposes and reflects information obtained during the committee's data gathering or from committee members' knowledge of the field. Such mention does not imply committee, National Research Council, or sponsor endorsement of any commercial product or service.

BOX 2-1
Illumina, Inc.: An Example of Convergence

The founding and growth of Illumina is a story of convergence that required the combined knowledge and talents of scientists, engineers, venture capitalists, and business managers—along with some good luck. Key ideas for Illumina's BeadArray technology were developed by David Walt and his laboratory at Tufts University from their research on fiber optic sensors and chemical monitoring. Their work, which started out using high-power lasers at Lawrence Livermore National Laboratory and small numbers of painstakingly made fibers, benefitted greatly from the development of cheap and robust optics components by the telecommunications industry. Similarly, independent developments in materials science enabled small reaction wells to be etched into a surface for optical interrogation. Parallel work on nucleic acid synthesis and bead-based combinatorial chemistry inspired the idea of "microarrays" of etched wells each containing a randomly deposited chemical probe bead with optical encoding. The high density, built-in redundancy, reproducibility, and flexibility of the new system made numerous applications possible (David Walt, personal communication).

Illumina was founded in 1998 with support from venture capitalists who recognized these attributes and the potential market opportunity in nucleic acid measurement. The company's continued success required convergence of science and technology depth with business expertise in market analysis and in the development of products and applications. One decision was to get involved in the international HapMap genotyping project cataloguing human genetic variation, which provided an opportunity for Illumina to demonstrate its technology. The acquisition in 2007 of the company Solexa also contributed to Illumina's ability to extend its technology. Solexa had developed nucleic acid sequencing by synthesis (SBS) derived from the earlier research of Shankar Balasubramanian, David Klenerman, and others at Cambridge University. The technology combined chemistry and informatics to read single bases of DNA as they were incorporated into a growing strand. The combination of Illumina's core BeadArray and SBS technologies in turn formed the foundation for the recent launch of the HiSeq X high-throughput sequencing platform, which is reportedly capable of generating up to 600 gigabytes of genomic data per day. According to the company, the HiSeqX Ten platform, combining 10 HiSeqX systems and designed for very large scale human genome sequencing, is now capable of reaching the $1,000 genome milestone, which has long been a goal of the life sciences community (Illumina 2014).

---

public policy, and enterprise management can also serve as a boon to the growth of convergent research and the fruition of its benefits.

To have an idea of how research convergence may play out in the future, it can be instructive to look at examples from the past. Molecular biology is an illustrative case. The need and opportunity to understand cell biological events at a chemical level resulted in the convergence of cell biology and biochemistry in the form of molecular biology. Today molecular biology is recognized as the unification of the knowledge domains and methods of its foundational disciplines to create a new discipline. What started out as interdisciplinary collaborations became dedicated molecular biology scientific conferences, grant programs, research journals, university departments, degree programs, new technologies and applications, and new industries. A contemporaneous advance in public policy, the Bayh-Dole Act of 1980, decentralized the control of federally funded intellectual property and heralded a proliferation of high-tech companies. Genentech, Amgen, and Genzyme are among the companies that dedicated themselves to the molecular biology convergence.

More recently, structural and functional genomics, mathematics, and computational science have transformed biology into an information science. By converging disciplines—including molecular biology, chemistry, optics, micron-scale manufacturing, combinatorics, and bioinformatics—genomics has catalyzed the development of further genome-scale research in such areas as proteomics and other "omics" fields. Genomics represents an acceleration of the convergence of biology with traditionally nonbiological disciplines like physics and engineering. Market leaders such as Illumina, Agilent, Affymetrix, and their commercial and academic forerunners have helped to advance this convergence, the full benefits of which have yet to be realized.

Systems biology builds further on the genomics-catalyzed transformation of biology into an information science as it incorporates not only engineering in practice, but also engineering design principles and control theory as a means to understand and predict the behavior of complex biological systems. Similarly, branches of mathematics and computer science that address the integration of disparate data types and the analysis and modeling of molecular and cellular networks are key contributors. The past 15 years have seen the creation of systems biology journals, grant programs, conferences, and education initiatives to meet the broader needs of the community engaged in this research, and systems biology has been incorporated into the biotechnology and pharmaceutical sectors. Merrimack Pharmaceuticals, for example, is a company premised on the idea that a systems-level understanding of cancer is important for the development of safe and effective therapeutics.

The ongoing convergence revolution in biology will bring more opportunities that can be translated into commercial and social successes. A likely example is the budding field of synthetic biology, which is in many ways a corollary to systems biology. If one can use engineering theories and design principles to understand and predict the behavior of biological systems, one can use this knowledge to design new biological systems with desired properties for a wide array of applications in health, energy, agriculture, manufacturing, environment, and information and computation. A critical demand of synthetic biology is the ability to make large numbers of new candidate components (e.g., genes) from which to construct biological entities. Startups like Gen9 and Ginkgo BioWorks are working to meet this convergent need.

2.5 CONVERGENCE STIMULATES THE BIOBASED ECONOMY

The final example of convergence in action focuses on its role in stimulating an innovation ecosystem that develops around and in partnership with an academic research center. Many convergence institutes and programs incorporate elements of entrepreneurship. For example, the University of California's Institute for Quantitative Biosciences (QB3) trains its graduate students and postdoctoral fellows on how to start companies and supports them with a concept called "startup in a box." Over the past 2 years, this service has reportedly helped students and postdoctoral fellows incorporate 140 companies, 35 of which are functional and rent space from QB3 for a nominal fee in low-cost facilities for small startups. QB3's

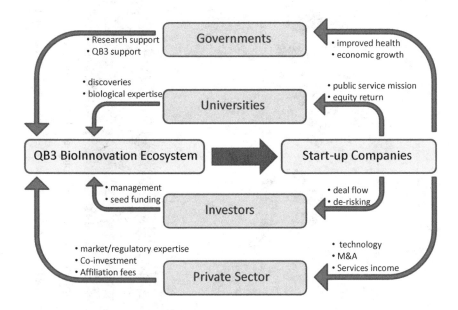

FIGURE 2-3 The convergence innovation ecosystem at QB3 involves dynamic interactions with government, university, and industry partners.
SOURCE: Courtesy of Regis Kelly, Director, California Institute for Quantitative Biosciences (QB3).

40

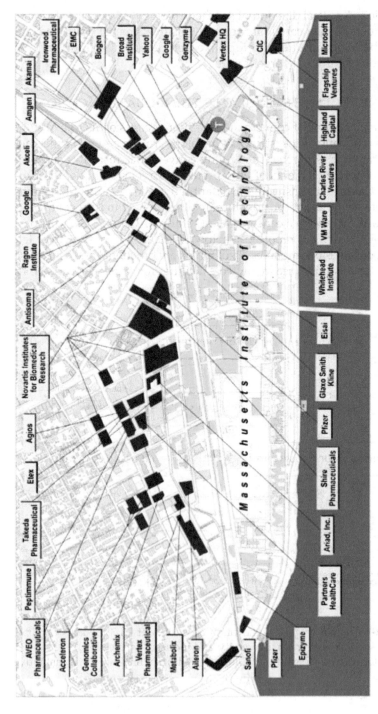

FIGURE 2-4 Multiple technology companies are located near MIT and form part of the ecosystem created and sustained by convergence.
SOURCE: Courtesy of Phillip A. Sharp, Institute Professor, Massachusetts Institute of Technology

incubator has created over 300 jobs and brought in $150 million from small business grants and angel and venture investments, reportedly for an investment by QB3 of $1 million (Kelly 2013). This interest is a consequence of QB3's efforts to create a community in which a wide range of stakeholders interact around developing new products and applications, and this ecosystem is helping to foster convergence in new ways (Figure 2-3). The Wyss Institute at Harvard University similarly reports that its researchers are judged not only on typical academic metrics such as journal publications but also on intellectual property, corporate alliances, licensing agreements, and a 5-year technology pipeline, resulting in an institute culture that is less like a traditional academic institution and more like a technology startup (Ingber 2013).

The inclusion in many convergence programs of a focus that spans discovery and application echoes the recommendations made in the ARISE II report on the need for integration across scientific disciplines as well as stakeholders (American Academy of Arts and Sciences 2013). It has been said that innovation moves through people connecting with each other and moving back and forth between a campus and nearby institutions where they can be creative (Sharp 2013). This phenomenon is demonstrated in the cluster of technology companies that have developed in the Boston metropolitan area around institutions such as MIT, Harvard, and Massachusetts General Hospital (Figure 2-4). Similar ecosystems, in which new companies have moved in or sprung up in association with academic centers, are also being formed around convergence hubs such as Stanford University and the University of Michigan North Campus Research Complex.

3

Convergence Is Informed by
Research Areas with Broad Scope

Many of the obstacles to effective convergence discussed in Chapter 4 have as much to do with interpersonal interactions as they do with science at the boundaries between disciplines. As a result, social and behavioral scientists who study human interactions, learning, collaboration, and communication as well interdisciplinary scholars who study new forms of knowledge creation and institutional structures and strategies have furnished valuable insights into the process of convergence and strategies to foster it.

3.1 TERMINOLOGY AND CONCEPTS

Convergence has characteristics in common with other terms used to capture the concept of research that spans disciplines. A foundation of research from social sciences, humanities, organizational theory, higher education studies, and studies of science and technology in society has deepened understanding of different kinds of integration defined in concepts of transdisciplinarity, interdisciplinarity, and multidisciplinarity. Although they have been understood in multiple ways by different groups, a core vocabulary is now accepted and consensus based within these research communities. It forms a basis of understanding of the challenges and implications that combining inputs presents, including theories, data, models, and methods from diverse disciplines. These definitions, which are not meant to be absolute, to be one size fits all, or to indicate the superiority of one mode over another, appear in Box 3-1. As

BOX 3-1
Definitions

The academic community that studies the process of research has developed terminology to describe different forms of knowledge creation within and across disciplines. For the purpose of this report and to provide a structure for discussions, the committee adopted the following definitions (based on a composite of Klein 2010a and Wagner, et al. 2011, extended to include Sharp and Langer 2011). An important shared characteristic is that various forms of research involving social and/or cognitive integration of knowledge cannot be distinguished readily at their boundaries. They are not absolute states, temporally or spatially, and multiple types of approaches to working within and across disciplines are needed in the research enterprise.

- *Disciplinarity* refers to a particular branch of learning or body of knowledge whose defining elements—such as objects and subjects of study, phenomena, assumptions, epistemology, concepts, theories, and methods—distinguish it from other knowledge formations. Biology and chemistry, for example, are separate domains typically segmented into departments in academic institutions.
- *Unidisciplinarity* is a process in which researchers from a single discipline, field, or area of established research and education practice work singly or collaboratively to study an object or to address a common question, problem, topic, or theme.
- *Multidisciplinarity* juxtaposes two or more disciplines focused on a question, problem, topic, or theme. Juxtaposition fosters wider information, knowledge, and methods, but disciplines remain separate and the existing structure of knowledge is not questioned. Individuals and even members of a team working on a common problem such as environmental sustainability or

Conceptual Degree of Integration

evident from the descriptions, many defining characteristics of convergence are similar or even identical to defining traits of transdisciplinarity, key among them merging of distinct and diverse approaches into a unified whole. The merging of expertise from fields of engineering with fields of physical and life sciences in order to create a new systems framework for integrative cancer biology is one example—bringing together areas such as experimental biology, computational modeling, and imaging technology.

Tremendous advances in knowledge and understanding have come from discipline-based scholars, and research within disciplines will continue to contribute to the advancement of knowledge. While there is evidence that incorporation of inputs from diverse fields of inquiry may a public health initiative would work separately, and their results typically would be issued separately or compiled in encyclopedic alignment rather than synthesized.

- *Interdisciplinarity* integrates information, data, methods, tools, concepts, and/or theories from two or more disciplines focused on a complex question, problem, topic, or theme. The scope and goals of research programs range from incorporating borrowed tools and methods and integrating them into the practice of another discipline to generating a new conceptual framework or theoretical explanation and large-scale initiatives. The key defining concept of interdisciplinarity is integration, a blending of diverse inputs that differs from and is more than the simple sum of the parts. Individuals may work alone, but increasingly research is team-based. Collaboration introduces social integration into the process, requiring attention to project management and dynamics of communication.

- *Transdisciplinarity* transcends disciplinary approaches through more comprehensive frameworks, including the synthetic paradigms of general systems theory and sustainability, as well as the shift from a disease model to a new paradigm of health and wellness. In the late 20th century, it also became aligned with problem-oriented research that crosses the boundaries of both academic and public and private spheres. In this second connotation, mutual learning, joint work, and knowledge integration are key to solving "real-world" problems. The construct goes beyond interdisciplinary combinations of existing approaches to foster new worldviews or domains.

Conceptual Degree of Integration

increase the likelihood of creative results, this does not mean research combining diverse inputs is on an evolutionary or deterministic path. Scientific advance has always been, and will continue to be, a combination of results from a multitude of incremental advances in knowledge and their verification with occasional notable breakthroughs of many different origins and arising from many different modes of knowledge creation: examples include serendipitous discoveries, eureka flashes of insight by individuals, and powerful integrations of knowledge from diverse fields by individuals and by teams. One challenge is to identify and understand the factors that influence the outcomes of research which successfully integrate diverse inputs, whether labeled interdisciplinary, transdisciplinary, or convergent. Another is to recognize that multiple types of approaches—including unidisciplinary, multidisciplinary, inter-disciplinary, and transdisciplinary—may occur simultaneously in a field or in an initiative because of the complex array of activities its participants undertake and diverse institutional contexts. As a result, disciplinary and interdisciplinary units, such as research centers, play complementary roles within many academic organizations.

3.2 MANY FACTORS AFFECT THE SUCCESS OF INTEGRATIVE AND COLLABORATIVE RESEARCH

Individual disciplines are associated with patterns of training and socialization, the ways that research questions are formulated, the meth-ods and conceptual models used to address those questions, and the manner in which knowledge is communicated. They help to promote instruction, research, scholarship, and assessment for their fields. Prior investigators have explored the nature of disciplines and characterized some of their similarities and differences. For example, Becher (1994) identified fields as falling into intellectual clusters consisting of the natu-ral sciences, science-based professions, humanities and social sciences, and social professions. But even within what might be categorized as basic sciences, characteristics typical of research conducted by a math-ematician (often working singly or with one or two others, and using theoretical and computational resources) and a chemist (often working as part of team of senior investigators, postdoctoral researchers, graduate students, and technicians and requiring a range of chemicals, instruments, and other equipment) can vary in significant ways.

In a university setting, discipline-based departments typically form the bedrock organizational structure. These units have a tradition of autonomy. However, over the course of the 20th century, a substantial intellectual history of inter- and transdisciplinary research and educa-tion arose. This history extends from problem-oriented research at the Social Science Research Council in the 1920s to large-scale interdisciplin-ary initiatives such as the Manhattan Project in the 1940s to the rise of new interdisciplinary fields in such diverse areas as molecular biology, women's studies, urban studies, environmental studies, and clinical and translational science. The scope of activities is wide: from the daily bor-rowing of tools, methods, and concepts across disciplinary boundaries to projects and programs focused on complex societal and intellectual questions, to the formation of new fields, interdisciplines, and transcend-ing "transdisciplinary" paradigms. In the latter half of the 20th century, boundary-crossing also became a recognized characteristic of knowledge production that was permeating disciplines, not simply a peripheral inter-est at the edges of "normal" work. The literature on institutional change

expanded in kind, with heightened attention to new organizational structures and management strategies along with new models of curriculum
and training. The literature on epistemological foundations of knowledge
expanded in turn, fostering new understandings of cognitive integration
while calling for expanded criteria of evaluation beyond discipline-based
metrics. Interdisciplinarity and collaboration also became increasingly
entwined, especially in scientific disciplines.

The amount of collaborative research that is undertaken (as captured
by simple but imperfect metrics such as coauthored journal papers) varies by field but has shown a pronounced increase over time. Science and
Engineering Indicators 2012 (NSF 2012) indicated that 67 percent of science and engineering (S&E) articles were coauthored in 2010 and papers
across all S&E fields had an average of 5.6 authors. Field-specific differences in degree of interaction persist, though. The report noted that "the
average number of authors per paper more than quadrupled [over the
period from 1990 to 2010] in astronomy (3.1 to 13.8) and doubled in physics (4.5 to 10.1). Growth in the average number of coauthors was slowest
in the social sciences (from 1.6 authors per paper in 1990 to 2.1 in 2010)
and in mathematics (from 1.7 to 2.2)" (NSF 2012, pp. 5-35). These results
echo the findings of a study of universities in Australia, New Zealand,
and the United Kingdom in which the authors observed that 96 percent
of articles published by faculty in the "science" cluster were coauthored,
compared to 14 percent of articles in the "arts" cluster, and that the average number of paper coauthors was larger for the sciences (Lewis et al.
2012). There is also some evidence that the trend toward interdisciplinary
research may reflect expansion of collaboration into fairly closely related
scientific disciplines (Porter and Rafols 2009). However, it is clear that the
number of authors per paper and coauthorship *per se* does not necessarily indicate interdisciplinary collaboation, nor does it substitute for more
complex descriptions of the substance of the work itself. Moreover, particular disciplines may dominate, and standard databases do not necessarily
account for the emergence of new interests and fields (Wagner et al. 2011).

While heterogeneity of fields can increase combinatorial opportunities
and contribute to the success of a research project by bringing together
diverse insights, such differences may also increase tensions among members (Boardman and Bozeman 2006; Nooteboom et al. 2007; Disis and
Slattery 2010). Since scientists from different disciplines are likely to have
different networks of peers, to participate in different conferences, and
to publish in different journals, their weaker social bonds may increase
the difficulty of developing goal interdependence and a sense of trust
(Cummings and Kiesler 2005). At least one study has found that a graph
of "cognitive distance" and collaboration success takes the form of an
inverted U, whereby optimal distance balances the benefits of knowl

edge diversity with the barrier to finding common collaborative ground (Nooteboom et al. 2007). This research focused on collaborative alliances among technology firms using measures such as patent data; thus, the extent to which the findings can be extended to academic researchers remains unclear. A survey of collaborative research experiences of academic investigators concluded that multidisciplinarity did not have a significant effect on collaboration success, but that outcome measures were negatively impacted when collaborations spanned multiple universities because of reduced opportunities for close coordination (Cummings and Kiesler 2005). However, the survey found no negative impact on projects that involved development of tools such as software, reflecting the complexity of factors involved in studying collaborative research.

The nature of the research question, norms among the fields involved, and individual characteristics and experiences of participants all influence outcomes in addition to institutional factors. Figure 3-1 summarizes the multiple factors that are involved. In *Creating Interdisciplinary Campus Cultures* (Klein 2010b), Klein also presents an overview of Barriers and Disincentives to Interdisciplinarity, as well as Facilitating Strategies and Mechanisms that are relevant to those that confront convergence initiatives (Klein 2010b, Tables 3.1 and 3.2).

The integration of disciplines that start from a point of fewer shared cultural characteristics would be expected to provide additional tensions that would need to be resolved, be it within a single laboratory or across a multi-investigator or multi-organizational team. For example, certain fields in the humanities and social sciences are dominated by individual scholars rather than structured into group laboratories, make greater use of single-author publications, draw largely on qualitative analysis, or have other disciplinary characteristics that may be less familiar to researchers practicing in the life, physical, medical and engineering sciences. The committee emphasizes that these differences do not mean that insights from these fields should not be integrated in convergent research, but that greater levels of cognitive dissonance among participants and greater starting differences in areas such as faculty expectations and organizational structures may factor in strategies used to support convergent initiatives. This caveat is affirmed in the formal distinction between Broad and Narrow Interdisciplinarity (Klein 2010a).

Despite the challenges recognized here, convergence efforts that merge insights from across life, physical, medical, and engineering fields integrate science disciplines that have several characteristics in common. This shared foundation helps provide a starting platform for development of the multilingual capacity and integrated research culture needed for convergence.

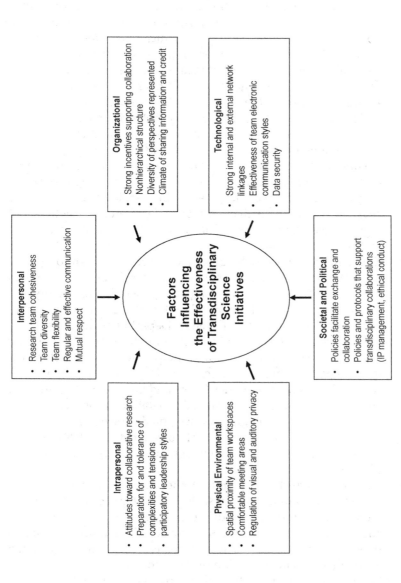

FIGURE 3-1 Factors influencing the effectiveness of transdisciplinary science initiatives. SOURCE: Adpated and reprinted from Stokols et al. 2008, with permission from Elsevier.

- **Research design and data collection**: Disciplines of life, physical, medical, and engineering sciences commonly draw on quantitative experimental data analysis and make use of individual case-study analysis or development of new theory less often than humanities and social sciences. Although there is a tradition of publishing clinical case studies in medical literature, a significant amount of basic biomedical research is undertaken by academic medical centers and a third of faculty at these centers report that they conduct basic science studies (Zinner and Campbell 2009).
- **Forms of knowledge dissemination**: Publication of peer-reviewed journal articles is a primary method of sharing research advances in these disciplines and is an important consideration in career advancement. Emphasis is also placed on participation in conferences as a forum in which developments may be shared prior to formal publication. Science and engineering disciplines vary in the relative weights given to different forms of knowledge sharing and in the details of article and conference practices, but together they share a base of norms on what it means to conduct and publish research.
- **Engagement in knowledge-transfer activities**: Although the extent varies, science and engineering disciplines also engage in knowledge dissemination through the generation of patents. For example, a study of the curricula vitae of 1,200 scientists affiliated with Department of Defense, Department of Energy, and NSF research centers found that mean patent rates were higher in computer science, engineering, and physical science fields than in biological science, although these fields were all higher than social science and humanities (Dietz and Bozeman 2005). In 2012, 96 percent of the U.S. journal article citations in issued patents were in five areas: biological sciences, medical sciences, chemistry, physics, and engineering. Biotechnology patents also made up the largest percentage of patents granted to U.S. universities in 2012 (NSF 2014).
- **Patterns of coauthorship and collaboration**: As discussed above, a majority of publications in science and engineering disciplines are now coauthored, although there remain disciplinary differences in the typical numbers of coauthors or number of disciplines cited in a given article. As noted earlier, coauthorship alone is not an adequate indication of the kinds of knowledge integration necessary for transdisciplinary collaboration, but may serve as a simplistic indicator of norms within these fields.
- **Traditions of open sharing as well as competition**: Some disciplines have a tradition of depositing prepublication papers in

open-access repositories (such as arXiv for physics and mathematics) or making use of open-source development strategies (for example, in the Linux operating system in the computational sciences).[1] In life sciences, norms as well as funding agency requirements call for the deposition of biological data such as nucleic-acid sequences and protein structures in databases such as GenBank or the Protein Data Bank, respectively, where the information is accessible to all researchers. However, legal questions surrounding patient consent and privacy complicate clinical information sharing in the medical field. Moreover, although there are both traditions and requirements for data sharing, competition to understand and make use of data is an important characteristic in many science fields.

Multiple case studies of interdisciplinary and collaborative research exist, particularly in the context of National Science Foundation (NSF)- and National Institutes of Health (NIH)-funded center programs. These case studies can provide further insight to inform the process of convergence in organizations. Examples include the following:

- *Knowledge and Distributed Intelligence Program (NSF)*: An analysis of 62 collaborations that received 3-year support through an NSF program in 1998-1999 suggested that collaborations involving investigators at multiple universities were associated with lower positive outcomes compared to single-university collaborations. Investigators reported a number of practical barriers to multi-university projects, including different university calendars and teaching schedules and negotiations over budgets and intellectual property. Institution-spanning collaborations were associated with reduced opportunities for information-sharing and coordination mechanisms such as face-to-face interactions, regular project meetings, co-taught courses, and direct faculty supervision of participating students, and the use of technology such as email did not fully overcome these barriers. The study suggested a role for longer-term funding for complex collaborations that recognizes the effort involved in undertaking such projects and the need for coordinating infrastructure (Cummings and Kiesler 2005).

---

[1] The Defense Advanced Research Projects Agency (DARPA) has recently announced that the source code for its supported projects will be available in the DARPA Open Catalog (DARPA 2014), reflecting this ethos within the software development community.

- *Transdisciplinary Research on Energetics and Cancer Centers (TREC) and Transdisciplinary Tobacco Research Use Centers (TTURCs) (NIH)*: To conduct an early-stage evaluation of centers in the NIH-funded TREC program, researchers developed a survey that analyzed participating investigators' orientations toward uni-, multi-, inter-, and transdisciplinarity and evaluated characteristics of proposals submitted for program development funds. The study reported that "perceptions of greater institutional resources at their TREC centers were related to a more positive outlook for a variety of collaborative processes and outcomes" (Hall et al. 2008, p. S170), suggesting that institutional investment can help facilitate the success of such endeavors. The TREC program includes a supporting coordination center, and it may be interesting to examine how this feature influences program outcomes as part of future assessments. A comparison of TTURC center awards with individual-investigator awards revealed that transdisciplinary teams demonstrated lower productivity during initial years of a project, but appear to become more productive and creative after a 3-year period (Hall et al. 2012), further supporting the longer-term nature of complex, collaborative efforts.

- *Comparison of the Texas Air Quality Study (TexAQS) and cross-center collaboration through the National Cooperative Program for Infertility Research (NCPIR)*: Environmental scientists from multiple partners (universities, federal laboratories, industry, and state bodies) and multiple sponsors were involved in TexAQS, which operated through a largely informal structure. Those engaged in the project undertook extensive planning, were in frequent communication, agreed on core aspects such as research questions, methodological approaches, and resource sharing, and generally already knew each other and had formed a sense of trust and competence. The NCPIR collaboration, on the other hand, was imposed by the funding agency, involved two geographically distant universities with researchers from basic and clinical fields who did not previously know each other and had different approaches to the research questions, and was in a scientific area (particularly polycystic ovary syndrome) that was still developing. Reportedly, "the result was that individual researchers conducted their own research (some of which was quite successful on an individual level), but the collaborative efforts of the group failed" (Corley et al. 2006, p. 991). The study highlighted how partners with similar cultures and relative scientific unity may share information more effectively to facilitate a positive group dynamic, while partners who approach research from different epistemic perspectives can encounter barriers even when more formal structures are in place and the research question falls broadly within the health sciences field.

In addition to case analyses such as those above, the Engineering Research Centers (ERC) program at NSF has created an online guide for scientists and academic leaders to provide information on factors to consider when establishing these centers (ERC 2014). Knowledge obtained from such program materials and from case studies that investigate the association of center attributes with metrics of success provides insights for existing convergence programs and useful guidance for developing new programs. The online Science of Team Science toolkit is another potential resource on the conduct and evaluation of team-based science. It is hosted by NIH (NCI 2014), which has also served as a sponsor and partner for annual Science of Team Science conferences (http://www. scienceofteamscience.org/). The committee especially looks forward to the results of a forthcoming National Research Council (NRC) study that is examining how factors such as team dynamics, team management, and institutional structures and policies affect large and small science teams. This study aims to capture the existing literature and wisdom of practice while illuminating gaps in the evidence base needed to improve team science processes and outcomes and to enhance collaborative research effectiveness. While the study focuses broadly on team-based science, it should provide valuable insights for convergence programs since these entail transdisciplinary integration of expertise, frequently undertaken in teams (NRC 2014). Finally, a large literature exists on how to foster interdisciplinarity in academic settings (Klein 2010b); the resources they provide for addressing barriers in organizational culture, faculty development, and program review can be adapted and extended to convergence.

3.3 REVISING STEM EDUCATION WILL FACILITATE CONVERGENCE

Science, technology, engineering, and mathematics (STEM) education has emerged as a key factor for facilitating the goals of convergence. The report *A New Biology for the 21st Century* suggested that "using biology to solve important problems could provide a platform to engage all students in the process of science, and illustrate the excitement and benefits of using science and engineering" (NRC 2009, p. 79). Complementing *A New Biology*'s recommendations on the role of life sciences in addressing broad societal challenges in areas such as food, health, and the environment, *Rising Above the Gathering Storm* (NRC 2007) and the *National Bioeconomy Blueprint* (White House 2012) highlighted the role of STEM education and entrepreneurship for enabling the knowledge economy, contributing to U.S. economic competitiveness, and training the bioeconomy workforce. Convergence approaches, which bring expertise from multiple fields to bear on innovative basic discovery as well as applied research and development, align closely with both of these goals. These reports furnish institutions considering how to foster an environment conducive to convergence with models and strategies for embedding this process into education and training programs.

Significant efforts have been made over the past decade to revise STEM education at the undergraduate and graduate levels, with particular emphasis on promoting training that makes interdisciplinary connections, incorporates problem-based learning and access to research opportunities, and draws on validated, evidence-based teaching methods (NRC 2003, 2012c; PCAST 2012; *Science* 2013). A recent report from the Association of American Medical Colleges and the Howard Hughes Medical Institute, *Scientific Foundations for Future Physicians* (AAMC and HHMI 2009), and new revisions to the medical school admission test, MCAT[2015], echo this trend. The revisions focus on demonstrating core competency in key biological concepts and draw on the integration of several fields, rather than on testing specific courses or disciplines in isolation. As the committee heard during its workshop, the environment provided by undergraduate liberal arts colleges and small, STEM-focused schools already models teaching and learning strategies that support the goals of convergence, through institutional policies that encourage faculty to develop new methods of teaching that span disciplines and because smaller physical size fosters random interactions that can lead to unexpected collaborations. These colleges send more students on to graduate training programs than would be expected based on their size (D. Singer 2013).

Revisions to STEM education also need to address the needs of the future workforce. At graduate and professional levels, the life sciences and biomedical workforce is diverse and continues to grow. Based on 2006 data, the biomedical research workforce included approximately 126,000 U.S. doctoral degree holders (approximately 64 percent male and 36 percent female) and over 63,000 foreign trained scientists. Twenty-six thousand were serving as postdoctoral fellows and an additional 25,000 were graduate students (NRC 2011b). Between 2000 and 2009, the largest increase in awarded science and engineering doctorates occurred in biological/agricultural sciences, medical/other life sciences, and engineering. In addition, the biological/biomedical, health sciences, and engineering areas received the largest allocations of academic research space and the largest new research space construction (NSF 2014). Meanwhile, career paths for science and engineering graduates are continuing to change, with reports on "best practices" and accreditation standards increasingly highlighting the importance of interdisciplinary and collaborative capacity. More than half of those who receive new doctorates across all academic fields now work outside of academia in industry, government, and nonprofit sectors and the number of professional science masters programs is increasing (NRC 2012a).

Recent reports have explored additional aspects of STEM education such as who participates in graduate science training, how long degree programs take, what percentage of students complete their degree, what types of training grants and funding sources support students, and what needs and opportunities exist for career paths to the workforce at both master's and doctoral levels. Several insights for fostering convergence emerge from these studies, including the increasing role of interdisciplinary and collaborative work in all stages and types of careers, the need to provide students with information on diverse career paths, the value of understanding of how to put research contributions into a broader context, and the role of skills such as communication and teamwork (Wendler et al. 2010; Wendler et al. 2012; NRC 2011c, 2012a, 2012d; NSF 2014).

The growing role of interdisciplinarity in the biological sciences, in particular, was highlighted in the most recent edition of the NRC assessment of doctoral programs. The rapid pace of development in biological and health sciences and the increasing interdisciplinary character of programs since the NRC's last assessment (in 1993) posed challenges to its classification methodology, which was largely based on an older taxonomy of discrete academic programs that did not recognize the emergence of new boundary-crossing interests and fields.

The report noted that, "although most doctoral work is still organized in disciplines, scholarly work in doctoral programs increasingly crosses disciplinary boundaries in both content and methods. The committee tried to identify measures of multi- and interdisciplinarity, but it believes it did not address the issue in the depth deserved, nor did the committee discover the kind of relation, if any, between multidisciplinarity and the perceived quality of doctoral programs" (NRC 2011c, pp. 105-106), concluding that this issue should be dealt with more fully in subsequent editions.

Viewed together, these and other reports affirm that possession of skill sets beyond disciplinary knowledge and research training are increasingly important for the success of students at all levels. A 2013 report on the role of "21st century skills" identified the related skills as clusters of competencies in cognitive, intrapersonal, and interpersonal domains that included aspects like creativity, flexibility, collaboration, and conflict resolution. Although this report was not able to definitively link such skills development during K-12 years with adult outcomes, it recommended expanding the evidence base for how to effectively teach and learn them and how to make them transferable (NRC 2013). The importance of skills that enhance research impact, including "communication, teamwork, relating work to a broader context, and application of research to larger corporate or social purposes" was similarly identified in recent reports on graduate school training from the Educational Testing Service and Council on Graduate Schools (Wendler et al. 2010, p. 44) and highlighted by participants at a workshop on graduate study in the chemical sciences (NRC 2012d). The types of 21st century skills identified by these reports all align with the skills that will be needed to work in a convergence environment, in which challenges are tackled across disciplinary boundaries through the integration of multiple areas of knowledge, and in which problem-solving may draw on the contributions of multiple team members and multiple partners within and outside of academia.

As academic institutions prepare their students for the research challenges and work environments they will likely encounter in the future and as they design education and training programs that incorporate new evidence-based teaching practices, all of these factors will be relevant. Beyond the reports already mentioned, institutions can also draw on guides such as the roadmap for interdisciplinary learning released by Project Kaleidoscope and the Association of American Colleges and Universities (Elrod and Roth 2012), which provide ideas for strategies to mobilize support, undertake pilot activates, define outcomes and assessment plans, undertake pilot activities, and sustain commitment. Other examples of strategies used by institutions to foster convergence at undergraduate and graduate levels are discussed in Chapter 4, along with some of the perceived challenges and needs for the future.

3.4 CONVERGENCE MAY CONTRIBUTE TO UNDERSTANDING QUANTIFICATION AND REPRODUCIBILITY IN LIFE SCIENCES

As the chapter highlights, a significant body of research has examined the relationship of individual and organizational factors to integrative and collaborative research and teaching, with insights that might transfer to the goal of fostering convergence. Discussion during the data-gathering workshop illuminated several additional differences in the ways that life scientists and physical scientists or engineers are perceived to approach problem solving, with potential impacts on fundamental research challenges at the frontier of the life, medical, physical, and engineering sciences.

Engineering fields generally approach challenges through quantification, since quantitative understanding of a system enables control. Quantification is becoming increasingly important in the biological sciences as well, and thus biologists increasingly need training in mathematics and computation. However, the living systems of interest in life sciences are complex, adaptive, and often not at equilibrium, making the mathematics required to model, analyze, and understand them extremely sophisticated. For example, modeling the signaling pathway of the epidermal growth factor receptor requires equations that cover 322 components and the 211 reactions in which they are involved (NRC 2011d). Effectively integrating an engineering approach to mathematical complexity into life sciences is a major goal for convergence that would help tackle the challenge of understanding and controlling biological systems, with results that would be applicable across questions in health, sustainability, and innovation.

Data reproducibility is another well-recognized challenge in the biomedical sciences. It has received wide attention due to pharmaceutical industry reports that results of published studies on cancer biology and drug targets could not be fully replicated (Prinz et al. 2011; Begley and Ellis 2012; related discussions appear in a special collection of *Nature* articles at nature.com/nature/focus/reproducibility). Numerous factors contribute to poor result reproducibility. Possible factors that have been suggested include limited ability to fully describe methods in written journal articles, uncharacterized variance in experimental conditions, limitations in preclinical cell culture and animal models, pressure on scientists to publish positive results, low value placed on replicating the results of others, and insufficient statistical expertise or experimental design. This is an area which needs further study in order to address a key stumbling block to research progress. Many believe that life and medical sciences have not focused as extensively as physics and engineering on developing common measurement standards and common guidelines for collecting data from biological samples. In order to move beyond information encoded in individual genomes to translational application, further attention to this challenge of standardization and reproducibility is required. Strategies adapted from the physics and engineering communities can contribute, although the complexity and individual variability of living organisms make measurement challenges in life and medical sciences unique. As one participant in the committee's workshop stated, "Let's figure out how to take the important biological processes and annotate them so that we're not simply accumulating data that's reproducible, but leading to knowledge that's actionable" (Dennis Ausiello, Workshop on Key Challenges in the Implementation of Convergence, September 16-17, 2013, Washington, DC). Convergence holds potential to contribute to the goal of incorporating rigorous measurement and analysis toolkits into life sciences while continuing to draw on the empiricism and observation that have formed the foundation for many life sciences advances of the past.

3.5 CONVERGENCE EXTENDS BEYOND THE INTEGRATION OF LIFE SCIENCES, PHYSICAL SCIENCES, MEDICINE, AND ENGINEERING

Most of the examples of convergence programs and institutes discussed in Chapter 4 were established around a core subset of life, physical, medical, and engineering sciences. However, many of the challenges these programs report encountering and strategies they have employed to foster convergence reinforce existing recommendations on how to nurture research that spans disciplinary boundaries more broadly. Where applicable, this report highlights similarities where information from convergence programs echoes such prior findings, notes aspects that may be specific to the combination of life, physical, medical, and engineering fields, and suggests how they affect challenges encountered in fostering convergence.

There is widespread recognition among scientists that addressing critical challenges in health, energy, and sustainability at both the research and application stages draws on contributions from disciplines beyond the life, physical, engineering, and medical sciences. Well-established areas such as cognitive neuroscience merge research in cellular biology and neural circuitry with behavioral studies to better understand complex human processes such as emotion. The economic and social sciences also make crucial contributions to the translation of innovations from fundamental research to widespread adoption. For example, "you can get engineers and use bio-fuels to build a great car, but people still have to buy it, it has to be priced. Behavior has got to play a big role. So I think that a true, complete solution to many of the problems we care about should include economics, psychology, behavior, sociology" (Carl Simon, Workshop on Key Challenges in the Implementation of Convergence, September 16-17, 2013, Washington, DC). The extent to which disciplines such as the social and economic sciences and humanities are being increasingly incorporated into an expanded concept of convergence and what additional cultural and institutional barriers this will present remains a matter of discussion, although the committee's view is that these fields have important insights to contribute in many areas of discovery and application.

4

Fostering Convergence in Organizations: Challenges and Strategies

Translating the "why" of undertaking convergence into the practical "how" of fostering it in individual institutional settings is a key question for the academic leaders and administrators whose responsibility this task will be. Institutions range widely in their missions, sizes, available budgets, and other characteristics with the result that no single template can be followed. The report draws largely, although not exclusively, from examples within academic institutions. It is important to recognize that national laboratories, nonprofit research institutes, industry, and other settings that contain experts from multiple disciplines in proximity to one another with access to facilities and instrumentation, and that contribute to the translation and implementation of research advances, are also relevant partners and are locations in which convergence can effectively occur.

This chapter explores areas where challenges are frequently encountered, identifies examples of strategies that have been used by different types of institutions and with different budget implications, and begins to articulate a set of cultural and structural characteristics linked to successful convergence programs. Many challenges encountered by convergence programs and strategies to address the barriers that arise echo those reported for facilitating interdisciplinary, transdisciplinary, or team science efforts more generally. Table 4-1 provides highlights of common challenge areas and indicates how the concepts apply to convergence. The subsequent sections of the chapter explore these and other areas further.

TABLE 4-1 Comparison of Perspectives on Common Challenges Encountered in Fostering Convergence

Common Challenge	Recommendations (NAS et al. 2004)	Perspective of this Report (2014)
Establishing effective organizational cultures, structures, and governance	Institutions should explore alternative administrative structures and business models that facilitate IDR across traditional organizational structures; institutions should develop equitable and flexible budgetary and cost-sharing policies that support IDR. Allocations of resources from high-level administration to interdisciplinary units, to further their formation and continued operation, should be considered in addition to resource allocations of discipline-driven departments and colleges.	Alternative structures must harmonize with the existing culture of investigator and laboratory autonomy. Convergent science fields provide a starting point to organize around compelling scientific and societal challenges. Factors such as differences in cost recovery models among schools of science, engineering, and medicine can complicate intra-university partnerships. Laboratories and core facilities are expensive to start up and maintain (see Sections 4.3 and 4.5).
Addressing faculty development and promotion needs	Recruitment practices, from recruitment of graduate students to hiring of faculty members, should be revised to include recruitment across department and college lines. The traditional practices and norms in hiring of faculty members and in making tenure decisions should be revised to take into account more fully the values inherent in IDR activities.	Promotion and tenure is still obtained through a primary departmental affiliation for many faculty members undertaking convergent research or associated with convergence institutes. Differences in faculty research and service expectations among science, engineering, and medical faculty may complicate collaborations, although multiple journal authors and diverse research contributors are already a norm within many science fields (see Section 4.4).

TABLE 4-1 Continued

Common Challenge	Recommendations (NAS et al. 2004)	Perspective of this Report (2014)
Creating education and training programs	Educators should facilitate IDR by providing educational and training opportunities for undergraduates, graduate students, and postdoctoral scholars, such as relating foundation courses, data gathering and analysis, and research activities to other fields of study and to society at large. Institutions should support interdisciplinary education and training for students, postdoctoral scholars, researchers, and faculty by providing such mechanisms as undergraduate research opportunities, faculty team-teaching credit, and IDR management training.	Curricula at the undergraduate level need to meaningfully integrate relevant physical, mathematical, computational, and engineering concepts and examples into life science courses and vice versa in order to provide a solid foundation for undertaking convergence. Opportunities are needed to effectively fill in gaps in training and expertise or to learn fundamentals of a new area to foster a common language and understanding. These opportunities are needed at the graduate, postdoctoral, and faculty levels (see Section 4.6).
Forming stakeholder partnerships	Academic institutions should develop new and strengthen existing policies and practices that lower or remove barriers to interdisciplinary research and scholarship, including developing joint programs with industry and government and nongovernment organizations. Continuing social science, humanities, and information science–based studies of the complex social and intellectual processes that make for successful IDR are needed to deepen the understanding of these processes and to enhance the prospects for the creation and management of successful programs in specific fields and local institutions.	Establishing extramural agreements is complex and may be affected by factors such as different leadership, funding, and cost-sharing models, or different traditions and expectations around issues such as patent development and intellectual property protection. Taking full advantage of the possibilities enabled by convergence increasingly draws upon contributions from fields such as the economic and social sciences, which have their own cultures and norms that must be considered (see Section 4.7).\

TABLE 4-1 Continued

Common Challenge	Recommendations (NAS et al. 2004)	Perspective of this Report (2014)
	Funding organizations should recognize and take into consideration in their programs and processes the unique challenges faced by IDR with respect to risk, organizational mode, and time.	Government support is one component of obtaining funding for convergence. Many convergence programs have also obtained critical support from sources such as private philanthropists and foundations interested in advancing science.
Obtaining sustainable funding	Funding organizations should regularly evaluate, and if necessary redesign, their proposal and review criteria to make them appropriate for interdisciplinary activities.	Income from startup companies and venture capital investors, which may be part of convergence ecosystems, may also provide support (see Section 4.8).
	Congress should continue to encourage federal research agencies to be sensitive to maintaining a proper balance between the goal of stimulating interdisciplinary research and the need to maintain robust disciplinary research.	

NOTE: As used in the table, IDR stands for interdisciplinary research. The prior recommendations cited in the table are drawn from NAS et al. (2004, pp. 5-7).

4.1 CONVERGENCE IS FACILITATED BY DEPTH AND BREADTH OF EXPERTISE

The focus of the committee's discussions and data-gathering was on fostering convergence in organizations, particularly in ways that interconnect and integrate the expertise of multiple investigators. Before turning to examples of these challenges and strategies, it is important to emphasize the characteristics of individual practitioners that facilitate convergence.

Convergence builds on a base of strong disciplinary research but demands that individuals be versed in multiple disciplines—for scientists to be "multilingual" citizens—to most effectively integrate a diversity of approaches to problem solving. The classic metaphor of T-shaped persons (Guest 1991)—those with an ability to collaborate across a broad set of disciplines, but who maintain a depth of expertise in a single field—is being extended to include π-shaped or comb-shaped skill sets that are

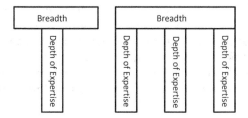

FIGURE 4-1 T and comb shaped individuals combine depth of expertise in specific areas with breadth to work across fields.
SOURCE: Committee on Key Challenge Areas for Convergence and Health.

invaluable for doing science in the 21st century (Figure 4-1). This does not imply that a scientist must obtain advanced degrees in multiple fields or, conversely, will be limited to being a "jack of all trades, master of none." A study of innovation at 3M explored roles within the company played by individuals exhibiting technical depth, breadth, or both qualities (Boh et al. 2014). The authors reported that individuals who functioned as successful system integrators developed deep expertise in core domains and extended their expertise over time as they understood how their domains interacted with other disciplines and they applied their knowledge to new challenges. "Thus, individuals learn to recombine existing components in novel ways while simultaneously building up new connections and new cognitive nodes of knowledge" (Boh et al. 2014, p. 356). Inventors in the company who had deep expertise were associated with more citations and patents, but inventors with both breadth and depth were associated with bringing value to the company by converting inventions into products. This type of multilingual fluency, developed over time, is at the heart of convergence.

Convergent research can also emerge from within individual laboratories and research groups, not only by bridging among them as part of larger-scale convergence initiatives. A research group may itself include members with a diversity of expertise and be tackling challenges at the boundaries of multiple fields. A common way in which a principal investigator (PI) brings new perspectives to his or her laboratory is by hiring a postdoctoral fellow or staff scientist who brings the skills to address an interesting new dimension of a research problem. Another tactic is by taking on a graduate student who brings to the program a different background. These are important strategies for fostering convergence. The individual backgrounds of the PI and research team members may also be cross-disciplinary in nature based on the combination of diverse educational and training experiences each has received. Over time, as new unified knowledge domains are created from the convergence of existing ones, individual persons and research groups with converged expertise will become the norm. An example is the discipline of molecular biology, which originated from cell biology and biochemistry but is now a unified discipline practiced by numerous individuals and research groups.

4.2 DIVERSE PERSPECTIVES SUPPORT INNOVATION

A central hypothesis of convergence is that diverse teams are able to generate innovative solutions to complex problems. Indeed, there is evidence that teams composed of individuals with different perspectives on problem solving will outperform groups that are more homogeneous in their approaches (Hong and Page 2004; Horowitz and Horowitz 2007). There is also evidence for increased creativity in more diverse teams (Stahl et al. 2010). Consequently, an environment where opinions—especially dissenting opinions—are openly expressed, where diversity is valued, and opposing ideas are respectfully communicated may be vital to the success of a convergence program. Such environments enable groups to think beyond embedded paradigms and collaborate to uncover creative solutions to difficult problems.

Diversity takes multiple forms, and a distinction can be made between diversity in problem-solving approaches (functional diversity) and diversity in demographic, cultural, and ethnic backgrounds (identity diversity). While both types are important for a successful future ecosystem of science and innovation, the latter appears to have a complex relationship with team performance. While identity diversity can lead to challenges in social integration and communication within a team, a group's perspective on diversity can mitigate and may even reverse these effects, yielding greater creativity and satisfaction (Stahl et al. 2010; Ely and Thomas 2001). As Section 3.2 discussed, functioning in an environment with diverse views and perspectives can be uncomfortable. Therefore, adopting inclusive attitudes toward diversity and using management strategies to foster diversity are essential for maximizing the return on investment of convergence efforts.

4.3 CONVERGENCE REQUIRES A CULTURE
AND SUPPORTING STRUCTURES

Developing an open, inclusive culture that values diversity, is flexible in the way it approaches problems, and has a common language is critical for success in any research effort that involves contributions from multiple disciplines. This process takes time. As one participant in the committee's data-gathering workshop noted, "We're five years into this initiative and I would argue that it will take another five years to actually get the kind of common language we need" (Anna Barker, Workshop on Key Challenges in the Implementation of Convergence, September 16-17, 2013, Washington, DC).

Leaders at multiple levels of an institution play significant roles in this process and in the ultimate success of convergence programs. A perceived focus on short-term financial considerations and administrative resistance to working through barriers to long-term convergent efforts is one obstacle identified during the committee's data gathering. Leaders who are committed to breaking out of academic divisions, willing to undertake the hard work of bringing people from different disciplines and partner organizations together, and supportive of policies that encourage convergent research are necessary. Because convergence takes different forms at different institutions, there is an opportunity to build from each institution's own strengths regarding personnel and leadership capacity at multiple levels. University presidents cannot make convergence happen by directive, just as an engaged group of faculty members cannot create a new transdisciplinary initiative without support from university leadership.

Who serves as the head of a convergence initiative also takes different forms in different places. At the Wyss Institute, for example, Donald Ingber is a core faculty member and continues to conduct active research, an attribute that he reports helps gain the respect of participating scientists. At QB3, which connects 220 laboratories across three university campuses, Regis Kelly has closed his own faculty laboratory to devote himself full time to the process of bridging academic domains and indicates that he could use more team members to contribute to this effort. And at the University of Michigan North Campus Research Complex, the university selected David Canter, a former senior vice president of global research and development at Pfizer, rather than a distinguished faculty member, to serve as the director.

A strong governance system is characteristic of the convergence programs the committee examined and it is important to be deliberate about developing governance for these complex efforts. At MIT, for example, the committee learned that members of convergence-focused institutes shared responsibility for deciding who joined the institution, how funding was secured, and how students and postdoctoral fellows were mentored (Sharp 2013). Convergence programs can be large undertakings and drawing on professional or nonacademic program management expertise can also play a useful role (Canter 2013; Ingber 2013). In addition to committed leadership and faculty, creating ample opportunities for individuals to share ideas, develop an understanding of disciplinary differences, and foster appreciation of the intellectual and technical contributions that different fields bring to bear on a problem is an essential component highlighted by many participants.

4.3.1 Strategy: Organizing Around a Common Theme, Problem, or Scientific Challenge

One mechanism institutions have employed to foster a shared sense of community and facilitate convergence is to organize an institute's or center's mission around core scientific problems that require a convergent approach to address. A few examples include the following:

- *Institute for Molecular Engineering, University of Chicago*: The Institute, established in 2011, focuses on understanding matter at a molecular level and using chemical, biological, mechanical, optical, and electrical building blocks to create functional systems that can address global issues. Its conducts research around current themes, which include Immuno-Engineering and Cancer, Molecular Engineering of Water Resources, and Quantum Information and Technology (University of Chicago 2014).
- *The Wyss Institute for Biologically Inspired Engineering, Harvard University*: The Wyss Institute, launched in 2009, is designed to foster innovation and technology translation by leveraging biological design principles to develop new innovations in engineering that address challenges in health care, sustainability, and other areas. Projects are organized around six enabling platform technologies: adaptive material technologies, anticipatory medical and cellular devices, bioinspired robotics, synthetic biology, biomimetic microsystems, and programmable nanomaterials (Ingber 2013).
- *Janelia Farm Research Campus, Howard Hughes Medical Institute*: The Janelia Farm Research Campus, which opened in 2006, represents an example in which a convergent research culture was created from the ground up outside the confines of an existing university structure. The campus is focused around two areas: identifying the basic principles by which nervous systems store and process information and developing new optical imaging technologies capable of imaging live systems at high temporal and spatial resolution (Rubin 2013).

4.3.2 Strategy: Implementing Management Structures Tailored to the Challenges of Convergence in Each Institution

Management factors have been shown to affect the success of research centers that bring together expertise across disciplines and organizations (Boardman and Ponomariov 2014). Convergence programs often involve faculty members and students from multiple fields, technical staff operating core facilities, program and business development managers, end-user partners like clinicians, and others with diverse skills and career trajectories. Different convergence initiatives employ different management structures to support their activities, based on their own organizational systems and goals. Some programs function as regular units of a parent university, while others operate as their own 501(c)(3) organizations. One descriptive example, drawn from the workshop, is below.

- *Wyss Institute, Harvard University:* The Institute is a 501(c)(3) non-profit organization that is owned by Harvard University but is governed by its own board of directors. The board is chaired by the Harvard provost and includes the deans of engineering and medicine, faculty representatives from the school of arts and sciences, the dean of engineering at Boston University, the CEOs of partner hospitals, industry representatives, and the Institute donor and his selected representatives. It includes an operating committee that makes resource allocation decisions, composed of the faculty who lead the Institute's six technology platform areas. It has also developed an Advance Technology Team of experts with industrial experience, who form a partnership with Institute faculty and help sustain institutional memory as products move through the stages of research and product development. Finally, the Institute includes an administrative management team with business development and startup experience. This structure reportedly works for Wyss as it leverages expertise from faculty who want their work to have impact, but who want to focus on the research side, and those with complementary business and manufacturing expertise. Wyss was not initially a separate 501(c)(3) organization—this change was driven by a need for greater independence from existing university constraints on issues such as hiring and salaries and became a condition for further funding from the primary donor (Ingber 2013).

4.3.3 Strategy: Fostering Opportunities to Interact Formally and Informally

Many methods can be used encourage spontaneous conversation and build connections among students and investigators across areas of expertise. Among the institutions and programs explored by the committee, communal activities used to break down interpersonal barriers included seminars, workshops, retreats, and parties. Several other possibilities are discussed in Section 4.5 on building design. Because faculty members are often busy with the demands of research, teaching, fundraising, and service commitments, a significant amount of collaboration appears to result from the connections students and postdoctoral researchers make among themselves that identify shared tools to address research challenges. As suggested below, students and younger researchers may be a particularly valuable source of ideas and energy for these events. It is worth noting that many of these types of activities can be implemented in a budget-conscious fashion:

- Graduate students and postdoctoral researchers can be empowered to share their knowledge with each other in peer-to-peer learning environments. At the MIT Koch Center, the Engineering Genius Bar serves as a place where biologists interact with and learn about tools and thought processes used by their peer engineers. The Koch Institute similarly has a "Doctor Is In" program that draws on the expertise of visiting physicians from Harvard, Dana-Farber Cancer Institute, or Massachusetts General Hospital (Jacks 2013; Sharp 2013).
- The Arizona State University Ignite program (Ignite @ ASU) is a student organization that organizes events "to gather, share ideas, connect with others and create change. It features rapid-fire 5 minute presentations that brings ASU students, faculty, staff and community members together to build more connected, vibrant communities" (ASU 2012; Barker 2013).
- Yale University and the Weizmann Institute of Science, Israel, are involved in joint research activities and have made efforts to incentivize student collaboration and innovation. A recent Yale–Weizmann Institute 'encounter' awarded small grants (on the order of $10,000) to self-assembled teams of students who proposed interdisciplinary, trans-institutional projects. The use of seed funding to catalyze convergent activities is discussed further in Section 4.8.

4.4 CONVERGENCE INTERSECTS WITH FACULTY STRUCTURES AND REWARD SYSTEMS

Many convergence initiatives are housed within universities and include faculty, postdoctoral researchers, and students as core participants. The configuration of academic institutions into subject-area departments is the bedrock of the current U.S. research infrastructure and traditional academic reward systems are based in disciplines. As a result, an institution seeking to foster convergence and implement structures to support it must consider what implications this goal will have for its current system. As Chapter 3 indicated, there are cultural similarities and differences among life sciences, physical sciences, and engineering that may influence the creation of such interconnections. Different institutions have addressed this challenge in different ways, but there are examples that can be considered by an institution whether it chooses to radically reevaluate its existing department structure or to maintain that structure and to establish policies that provide bridges across it.

4.4.1 Strategy: Radical Reorganization

A few organizations that support convergent research have undertaken radical reorganizations of department-based university systems or have been established outside traditional academic structures:

- *Arizona State University (ASU)* implemented significant changes to its organizational structure in order to embed the concept of convergence as a foundational element. Within 2 years of arriving at ASU, president Michael Crow had dissolved almost all of the existing academic departments and in their place created 23 new schools and initiatives such as the Beyond, Biodesign, and Complex Adaptive Systems Institutes. The goal of this effort was to create a new ecosystem to foster knowledge building and use-inspired research that was very different than a department-based structure (Barker 2013).
- *Janelia Farm Research Campus,* funded by the Howard Hughes Medical Institute (HHMI), involved constructing an entirely new institution for convergent science. The approach did not require changing an existing culture but rather creating a new one with no departmental affiliations or tenure. Janelia Farm scientists do not seek external funding and are required to be on-site 75 percent of the time so that they are available for collaboration. Janelia's approach attracts individuals who are willing to take a risk for a potentially high payoff from working in a transdisciplinary

environment in which half the people had initial training in biology and the others had training in physics, computer science, and engineering along with a sizable percentage from industry. Each lead researcher has a small group that shares resources and collaborates with other groups by combining skills to tackle common problems. Reportedly, when HHMI was in the process of creating Janelia Farm, many researchers commented that the facility would have difficulty attracting top talent because of the lack of a tenure mechanism. Instead, the organization views the lack of a tenure track as a filter for those who would not fit the culture that HHMI was creating. Since it opened, Janelia Farm has attracted researchers who gave up tenure at major universities along with scientists from industry who wanted to work in an academic environment without the pressure to generate publications and obtain outside funding that is required by tenure-granting institutions (Rubin 2013).

The example of the Janelia Farm Research Campus and similar types of non-profit research institutes provides an interesting case to consider when thinking about the broader implications of models for fostering convergence and how they might scale. Janelia itself has no disciplinary departments and tenure structure, but relies on the infrastructure of university-based training programs to produce those with the interests and skills to thrive in the type of collaborative environment it has created. As a result, multiple and complementary models to foster disciplinary and convergent research will be needed in the overall research enterprise. The example also highlights the important role of education and training programs to produce future convergence participants (see Section 4.6).

4.4.2 Strategy: Working With and Across Existing Departments

With the exception of institutions such as ASU that have eliminated traditional department structures or organizations such as Janelia Farm or the Institute for Systems Biology[1] that were established outside of such environments, most universities and research centers maintain a department-based system. Finding successful ways to leverage the knowledge within disciplines and to navigate the relationship between departments and convergence programs is therefore a critical part of the success of such programs.

Interdepartmental institutes and centers that can be nimble in their

---

[1] For a description of the Institute for Systems Biology, see http://www.systemsbiology.org/.

focus are one option for supporting convergence within a university framework that includes disciplinary departments. Jacobs (2013) reports that the top 25 research universities in the U.S. average more than 100 research centers, many of which are organized in discipline-crossing ways. Many research universities are thus hybrids of discipline-based departments and structures that cross various boundaries.

To be successful, however, mechanisms that address faculty hiring, cost sharing, and other logistical challenges need to be considered. If researchers and administrators feel that the motivating philosophy of convergence attacks the primacy of the individual investigator, this can provide one potential barrier to success. Fernando Martinez of the University of Arizona's BIO5 noted that faculty members sometimes voice a concern that convergent research diverts funding from investigator-initiated basic research or that it is primarily product oriented rather than knowledge oriented in nature. He views this as a false dichotomy and reported that BIO5 works to emphasize convergent research as a different form of the academic culture of individuality and autonomy, which are essential for creativity, and as part of the knowledge development continuum (Martinez 2013). Other examples of how programs have addressed these challenges include the following:

- *Bio-X, Stanford University:* Bio-X is one of 18 interdisciplinary institutes at Stanford that each have a dean equivalent to those of the university's schools, resources including program and education funds and laboratory buildings supported by annual budgets allocated from a central university fund, and together form a matrix crossing the university. Strong departments and schools are reportedly a necessity for Bio-X and the other institutes since hiring and promotion remains the function of these units, though it is possible to provide incentives for departments to hire faculty with certain skills or experience. To support departmental engagement and bridge-building and to encourage faculty to accept the convergent research paradigm, program funds are not obtained by "taxing" participating schools or departments. An evaluation of the Bio-X program, conducted by Daniel McFarland and Woody Powell of the Stanford School of Education, found that interactions among faculty across the university increased dramatically in the years since Bio-X was established. An interactome plot reveals that Bio-X has created a horizontal web that stretches across school and departmental boundaries (see Figure 4-2) (Shatz 2013).
- *Wyss Institute:* All Wyss Institute faculty members continue to hold academic appointments in their home institutions and

1995-97 Before Bio-X   2005-07 After Bio-X

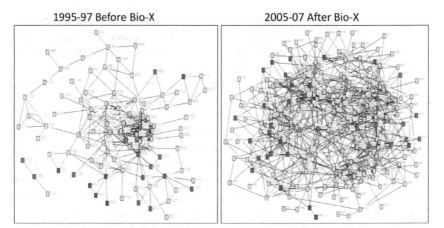

FIGURE 4-2 The web of faculty interactions created by Bio-X. The network of faculty interactions across Stanford has expanded since the establishment of the Bio-X program. The resulting network reportedly appeals to technology companies who want access to a range of faculty and their expertise. An additional reported benefit is the creation of a generation of young scientists who are comfortable working in convergent environments and who are in high demand in both academia and industry.
SOURCE: Courtesy of Daniel McFarland, Professor, Stanford University.

departments or schools and to meet the requirements of those departments in addition to those of the institute. This is a common practice at many convergence institutes. Though this can be an extra burden, it means that anyone who joins the institute is committed to its mission. Almost all institute members maintain their original laboratories and no faculty member has dedicated space at the Wyss Institute; space is allocated to projects, not to individual faculty. As reported during the workshop, this balance enables participating faculty to maintain the unique cultures of their own laboratories while benefitting from the strong transdisciplinary culture of the institute. The Wyss Institute also conducts co-recruitment of faculty with academic deans and department chairs, and reports that combining recruitment in this manner serves as a major attractor. Institute faculty are on 3-year renewable appointments that can be terminated, in which case the faculty member would return to his or her home department (Ingber 2013).

- *The Lewis-Sigler Institute for Integrative Genomics, Princeton University:* The Lewis-Sigler Institute houses 12 to 15 research groups and also includes nonresident affiliated faculty. Faculty members hold their tenure and tenure-track appointments in participating university departments including molecular biology, ecology and evolutionary biology, physics, chemistry, computer science, and chemical engineering. The Institute also supports early career scientists as 5-year Lewis-Sigler Fellows (Princeton University 2013).

- *Christopher S. Bond Life Sciences Center, University of Missouri:* The Bond Center involves the participation of 41 faculty investigators who hold appointments in 12 academic units drawn from the Colleges of Agriculture, Food and Natural Resources; Arts & Science; Engineering; Human Environmental Sciences; Veterinary Medicine; and the School of Medicine. The Center's website states that "as a requirement for membership in the Bond Life Sciences Center, researchers have agreed to exploit opportunities for novel research approaches via collaboration with LSC colleagues and others. In return, the LSC shares salary support of LSC investigators with their academic units and offers state-of-the-art facilities and a seed grant program to foster innovation" (University of Missouri 2014).

Regardless of whether or not they establish formal institutes and centers, institutions can encourage teams of researchers to come together in a more ad hoc manner, to develop ideas to attack with convergent science approaches, and to operate on ground rules that the team sets. To foster such a strategy, institutional incentives include catalytic seed funding, workspace, and perhaps access to core facilities. Examples of project-based seed funding incentives that have been employed by institutions to encourage convergent research are discussed further in Section 4.8.

Cluster hiring, where departments work together to coordinate hiring of faculty who will participate in convergent activities, can be an additional budget-conscious tool for supporting the growth of such programs. By bringing on board a cohort of several faculty members around a theme, cluster hires can enable a convergence initiative to get under way faster and can help shift institutional cultures toward a collaborative mindset. For example, at the University of Arizona cluster hires have reportedly occurred or are occurring in three areas that complement existing strengths: the merger of information technology and plant sciences, imaging and microscopy, and targeted drug development (Martinez 2013). Many other universities have undertaken cluster hiring initiatives to foster interdisciplinary research, including the University of Wisconsin-Madison (2014a) and the University of Iowa (2014), and to build capacity in specific scientific areas, such as the Penn Nano Cluster-Hiring Initiative

(University of Pennsylvania 2014). Even using a strategy of cluster hiring, however, many faculty continue to obtain tenure through a home department and therefore academic promotion and tenure processes will need to account for convergent research.

4.4.3 Strategy: Embedding Support for Interdisciplinarity in the Promotion and Tenure Process

As was made clear by examples such as HHMI's Janelia Farm, researchers are willing to work in novel environments to engage in convergent research, even without the option of tenure. However, concerns over adequately accounting for participation in convergent research during promotion and tenure decisions remains a topic of great interest for many scientists working at convergent interfaces. A reward structure that emphasizes individual investigator-driven research and publication and questions of how credit is assigned for multi-investigator-led projects represent widely acknowledged challenges to any form of interdisciplinary or collaborative research, including convergence (see Box 4-1).

Institutions will need to provide clear guidance to support faculty engaged in convergent research. Universities can include expectations of collaboration during the hiring process and department leadership can make recommendations to young faculty regarding team-based projects in which they are participating. This establishes a basis for collaborative work. Tenure and promotion committees will also need guidance that enables them to fairly evaluate convergent as well as unidisciplinary research, teaching, student mentorship, and service efforts. One concrete step that can be taken toward addressing obstacles to convergent research is for tenure and promotion committees to adopt specific criteria that recognize contributions to such activities. Tenure and promotion committees can also solicit letters from faculty members' senior collaborators, something that is not done traditionally, or ad hoc committee members outside a primary department could be appointed to evaluate the faculty member's convergent research. Funding agencies may be able to contribute as well by including language in requests for proposals indicating that collaborative outputs such as coauthored journal articles are appropriate products. When making promotion and tenure decisions, a faculty member's impact in the research community beyond outputs such as papers and patents, such as changing an approach to a problem or opening up new avenues of investigation, should also be considered. New types of reward mechanisms might even be envisioned, although further evidence of the impact of such prizes and awards would need to be explored (see Box 4-2). Messages from university leadership as well as formal policy changes may be required, particularly if there is a real or perceived bias

---

BOX 4-1
Promotion and Tenure Policies

Traditional academic promotion and tenure language generally focuses on individual scientific achievement and lacks explicit criteria for demonstrating and evaluating contributions from convergent research, particularly contributions made as part of team efforts. Typical promotion and tenure language may also be less well adapted to assessing activities that extend beyond basic science discovery to translational application, which is a common feature of convergence activities. The need for institutional policies that address boundary-crossing and/or collaborative research such as that represented by convergence is a well-recognized challenge (NAS et al. 2004; NRC 2005b; Klein 2010b). As reported to the NRC Committee on the Science of Team Science, a survey of promotion and tenure language from 42 responding institutions that received National Institutes of Health (NIH) Clinical and Translational Science Awards revealed that a quarter did not have language specific to collaborative, interdisciplinary, or team science. The remaining 32 institutions recognized these types of activities in various ways, such as by recognizing that interdisciplinary or team science plays a role in advancing science or by addressing how to demonstrate contributions when assembling a promotion and tenure dossier (Hall 2013).

Guidance and best practice suggestions for promotion and tenure processes are available from groups such as the Computing Research Association and the Council of Environmental Deans and Directors (Pollack and Snir 2008; NCSE 2014). Individual universities also provide examples that can be drawn on or adapted. The 2013 manual from the University of Southern California's Committee on Appointments, Promotions, and Tenure (USC 2013), for example, includes sections specific to interdisciplinary research and collaborative research. In part, these include the following:

> Department and School committees evaluating interdisciplinary work should try to value appropriately publications outside of the home discipline and its usual journals. In evaluating the candidate's teaching and mentoring activities, they should consider interdisciplinary graduate teaching and co-teaching, as well as advising or co-advising graduate students outside the home department. The committee should make special effort to understand other disciplines' customs on co-authorship, sequence of authors, and the use of conferences, journals, or monographs as premier outlets.

> UCAPT will use appropriate flexibility in reviewing interdisciplinary dossiers. UCAPT sits in disciplinary panels and can assign a dossier to a different panel or can use mixed panels, ad hoc committees, or special consultants as needed (USC 2013, section 2.9(c), pp. 13-14).

---

on tenure and promotion committees against team-based science or dismissal of contributions to a team-based project, grant, or paper. At the same time, faculty members must be able to clearly explain the roles they play in convergent research efforts that involve multiple participants. Two examples drawn from the workshop illustrate the challenges:

BOX 4-2
The Film Industry: A Model for Rewarding Convergence?

The creation of a motion picture is a transdisciplinary undertaking involving the efforts of writers, actors, photographers, editors, costume designers, lighting and set technicians, publicists, marketers, and film distributors. Through the Oscars, the industry recognizes excellence in individual achievement (i.e., best actor or best screenplay) as well as collective accomplishment (best picture) and lifetime excellence (a lifetime achievement award). Major scientific awards like the Nobel Prize generally recognize breakthroughs made by individual researchers and their laboratories. Nobel Prize traditions, for example, stipulate that only a maximum of three laureates may share an award. Is there a role for a new type of award or event honoring collective achievement in science? Would this bring new recognition to those who excel in convergent research and provide new role models for this form of innovation?

- *Parker H. Petit Institute for Bioengineering and Bioscience (IBB):* IBB, established in 1995, involves the participation of approximately 130 faculty associated with multiple departments on the Georgia Tech campus. Faculty members at the Petit Institute hold their academic, tenure-track appointments in one of these participating academic departments. As Robert Nerem reported, "we changed the promotion and tenure process so that the first thing that a department P&T committee can do is appoint what we call an area committee, or sometimes the first level committee, which is supposed to be the three to four faculty on campus who can best evaluate the scholarship research activities of the faculty member. And that has been an important addition to our P&T process" along with a process in which any areas of disagreement with the area committee report by the department, college, or provost are substantively addressed (Robert Nerem, Workshop on Key Challenges in the Implementation of Convergence, September 16-17, 2013, Washington, DC).
- *University of Arizona, BIO5:* Fernando Martinez reported that creating a parallel promotion and tenure process by simply juxtaposing a member of BIO5 with the departmental faculty was a strategy that did not work at the University of Arizona. Rather, to be most successful the promotion and tenure system for the academic structure as a whole system needed to buy in to the concept that convergence research is an essential strategy to solve problems.

Discussions during the committee's data gathering identified the existence of a generation gap between students and younger faculty and senior academics and leaders. It has been suggested that the need to obtain tenure and funding pushes younger faculty to be disciplinary in research focus or impedes them from devoting significant efforts to forms of transdisciplinary research such as convergence until they are more established. However, many younger scientists at the workshop expressed the expectation that convergence is a normal process for how things are done. In their own research and their own laboratories, these scientists already approach problems in a highly integrated manner, have skill sets that span traditional boundaries, are comfortable working with others who have expertise in diverse areas, and want to be part of a research system that includes contributors such as clinicians and industry in order to link fundamental science with translational products and services. The committee does not have data to address whether the success of science, technology, engineering, and mathematics (STEM) education efforts on problem-centered learning and hands-on research experiences; changes in the ways younger scientists approach communication and collaboration; the popularity of interdisciplinary majors such as bioengineering; career stage in which thorny partnership issues in logistics, legal and intellectual property arrangements, and cost sharing have not been encountered; or some combination of these and other factors contributes to this mindset. This would be an interesting question for further analysis. Nevertheless, this attitude is a positive sign for the future of convergence and institutions should have opportunities to build on the enthusiasm of their students and younger faculty.

4.5 FACILITIES AND WORKSPACES CAN BE DESIGNED FOR CONVERGENT RESEARCH

The relationship between space, collaboration, and productivity is complicated. As Figure 3-1 emphasizes, physical environment is one factor among many that affect the success of convergence efforts and the interacting effects of organizational culture, management, and individual characteristics cannot readily be separated or prioritized. Researcher proximity and the use of spaces that facilitate chance encounters can lead to increased consultations and collaborations and may impact outputs such as co-authored papers. For example, one study of university research centers suggested that researchers from centers with unbroken, co-located office and laboratory space reported an "innovation outcome" measure higher than researchers from centers occupying split spaces (Toker and Gray 2008).

Many of the convergence institutes that have arisen over the previous decade include dedicated physical space designed to facilitate interactions among students and faculty that cross disciplinary boundaries. When designing the physical buildings that house convergent research efforts, some institutions incorporate modular laboratory spaces that could potentially be reconfigured in the future to match changing research needs. Reportedly, this type of space flexibility was part of the design of the BioFrontiers Institute of the University of Colorado, where researchers are assigned space based on interests rather than by departmental affiliation and each space is sufficient to house the equipment, students, and staff associated with several laboratories (University of Colorado 2014). It is also a feature of the Discovery Building at the University of Wisconsin, which houses the Wisconsin Institute for Discovery (part of the University of Wisconsin-Madison Graduate School, a public university) and the Morgridge Research Institute (a private, nonprofit organization) (University of Wisconsin-Madison 2014b). Adapting laboratory space to new configurations of wet and dry research may pose particular challenges for convergence across life, physical, medical, and engineering fields, since customizing a laboratory at startup may cost millions of dollars (Shatz 2013). Nevertheless, design strategies that offer future flexibility may be particularly relevant for convergence institutes since they are conducting research at the frontier of fast-developing fields. Building renovations also offer institutions valuable opportunities to consider new configurations of researchers, and may be financially more feasible for institutions than constructing entirely new spaces.

The community-building role of supporting infrastructure in convergence facilities, such as cafeterias, coffee areas, and lounges, is also frequently mentioned as providing crucial opportunities for faculty, staff, and students to interact outside of planned activities (Hollingsworth 2002; Jacks 2013; Shatz 2013; Nerem, Workshop on Key Challenges in the Implementation of Convergence; University of Colorado 2014). In the life, physical, medical, and engineering fields, core facilities that house shared instruments and research technologies are common and may provide a similar type of communal venue. Access to sophisticated core facilities may be a particularly useful incentive for convergence, and the need for support for such core spaces has been noted in prior reports.[2] Several other strategies that institutions have incorporated in the physical spaces that support convergence are described below.

---

[2] One of the recommendations from the ARISE II report is to "Expand support for shared core research facilities (especially those that span multiple PSE [physical sciences and engineering] and LSM [life sciences and medicine] approaches), including funding for stable appointments of professional staff to direct them" (American Academy of Arts and Sciences 2013, p.21).

4.5.1 Strategy: A Central Location in Relation to the Rest of the Campus

Bio-X at Stanford University, created in 1998, is a university-wide institute that includes the participation of over 600 faculty members drawn from almost all of the university's schools. The Clark Center, which opened in 2003, is the official home of Bio-X and houses its 44 core faculty members. The Center sits at the intersection of the science campuses at Stanford and is a 5-minute walk to the medicine, chemistry, biology, physics, and engineering buildings, enabling the Center to function as both a physical and intellectual hub for the Bio-X community (Shatz 2013).

4.5.2 Strategy: Arranging Laboratories and Common Spaces to Maximize Interactions

The University of Michigan examined how the design of facilities affects collaboration through a study conducted by investigators in its School of Social Sciences. The results indicated that the amount of path overlap between investigators as they went through their day strongly correlated with the likelihood of collaboration (Figure 4-3) (Kabo et al.

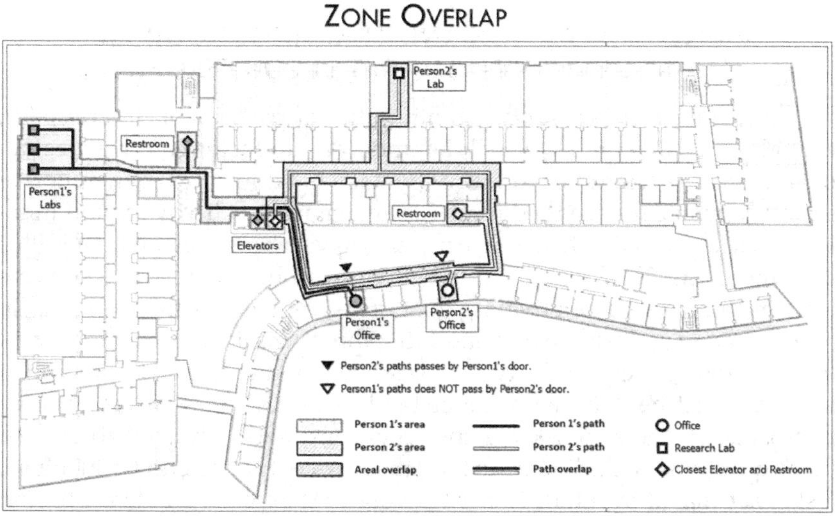

ZONE OVERLAP

FIGURE 4-3 The effect of path overlap on research collaboration. The amount of physical overlap in a biomedical research building at the University of Michigan— the relative position of offices, how close two investigators were to the coffee pot, and other factors of proximity—were strongly correlated with the likelihood that collaborations would form.

SOURCE: Kabo et al. 2013. Reprinted by permission of SAGE Publications.

2013). Other convergence programs that have used facility design with a goal of encouraging investigator overlap include the following:

- The building that houses the Institute for Bioengineering & Bioscience at Georgia Tech, completed in 1999, was designed to enhance opportunities for chance meetings including through co-location of researchers and the use of shared core instrumentation facilities. Research is organized into "neighborhood" clusters that include faculty and students from multiple disciplines, and space in the building is assigned based on research interests rather than by department (Nerem, Workshop on Key Challenges in the Implementation of Convergence; Georgia Tech 2014).
- In MIT's Koch Institute for Integrative Cancer Research, each research floor includes a mix of biological sciences and engineering laboratories. Spaces regularly accessed by all researchers, such as bathrooms and elevators, are located within a "racetrack" corridor that loops the floor, forcing scientists to leave their laboratories during the day. The building also contains 22,000 square feet of shared core facilities spread throughout the building that comprise the Swanson Biotechnology Center (Jacks 2013).

4.6 NEW EDUCATION AND TRAINING PROGRAMS CAN BE DEVELOPED TO FOSTER CONVERGENCE

To sustain and expand the communities of participants interested in engaging in convergence, it will be important to foster convergence not only in today's scientific workforce but also to build a next generation of scientists who embrace the process as an avenue for discovery and innovation. Scientists will always face increasingly complex research questions and the questions of today will likely pale in complexity with those that arise in the future. A motivating goal of convergence is the view that to address many of these current and future problems at emerging interfaces between disciplines, a new type of scientist will be needed. This type of scientist must be "one who understands a broad range of disciplinary approaches, is able to ask creative questions, and is trained to answer those questions with diverse tools. This 21st-century scientist must have a skill set that allows him or her to probe and explore problems, to find and critically evaluate information, to work productively as a member of a team, and to effectively communicate research findings to others" (Colgoni and Eyles 2010, p. 10). To meet this challenge it will be imperative for the higher education system to design, implement, sustain, and evolve undergraduate and graduate educational programs that effectively promote student learning that transcends traditional disciplinary boundaries and that promotes a culture of scientists who see convergent approaches to complex scientific questions of the future as one critical strategy.

While there is a significant body of research articulating the value of an interdisciplinary approach to science teaching and student learning, interdisciplinary science education still fits awkwardly into an academic structure that is layered into discipline-based departments often scattered across a campus's geography. Therefore, it will take intentional efforts to achieve success given the profound changes that have taken place in the nature of the life sciences and in how complex, convergent research is performed and communicated. In order to achieve success, universities and colleges will need to reexamine current courses and teaching approaches to see how to best meet student needs. For example, new educational approaches in life sciences must address the importance of building a strong foundation in mathematics and in physical and information sciences to prepare students for research that is increasingly quantitative and data intensive in character. The implementation of new approaches will also need to be accompanied by a parallel process of assessment to verify that progress is made toward the institutional goals of student learning. A critical challenge facing education in field after field is how to provide sufficient knowledge in primary areas of expertise, as well as sufficient knowledge to interact at the frontiers of research challenges that cut across disciplines, in a reasonable time frame.

The overall mission of curriculum design at the undergraduate level is to provide all students, regardless of their intended majors, with an integrated foundation of knowledge. When addressing the challenges of designing an interdisciplinary, convergent educational program, a key first step is to define the objectives of the curriculum in a way that balances the trade-off between depth of knowledge and breadth of knowledge. Some goals for undergraduate student interdisciplinary learning, regardless of field, are

- to develop in students the intellectual capacity to deal with real, complex problems;
- to build student confidence and willingness to approach problems from multiple perspectives;
- to build student ability to communicate with scientists from other disciplines;
- to develop student ability to make decisions in the face of uncertainty (reflective judgment); and
- to help students understand strengths and limitations of different disciplinary perspectives.

To accomplish these goals, learning should be goal-directed, exciting, and personal. A problem-solving approach pushes the evolution of curricula and keeps courses fresh, a benefit for both students and faculty. Problem-solving approaches can also be an effective way to help students learn how to work in teams. An important consideration when using this type of team-based, problem-solving strategy is to form student teams that are diverse in terms of educational and personal background, to provide practice opportunities to collaborate in such environments and because research has shown that teams that include a diverse mix of individuals may be more likely to succeed.

One aspect of the balancing act of curriculum development necessary to support convergence is to take into account how much physics, math, statistics, or engineering a biologist needs to learn in formal class settings versus through informal contacts and through training that occurs as a member of a research effort involving colleagues from multiple disciplines. The same is true for those starting from areas of physical sciences and engineering who need to understand biological concepts. Colleges and universities have made efforts to revise undergraduate education programs to tackle some of these challenges, particularly the issue of how better to integrate mathematics and quantitative science into biology. Two examples drawn from the workshop are below. Whatever approach is used, achieving support for new curricula across the entire institution is critical in order for it to be embraced and sustained.

- The NEXUS Physics course at the University of Maryland arose from an effort to make connections between disciplines more explicit, particularly the relationship of physical principals to understanding biological systems. The course underwent several rounds of development that highlight the difficulty of designing an integrated course. Initially, biologists and biophysicists proposed a curriculum but the physics department objected based on information from the pedagogical literature on effective physics teaching. Gathering a large group of biologists, physicists, and university administrators failed to reach consensus on course content. The most successful strategy was to use a small core group of biologists, physicists, and one university administrator, to focus on cross-cutting topics, to draw in additional faculty perspectives as needed, and to make content available using a wiki. Although a challenge to develop, having a community of faculty invested in the outcome may contribute to course sustainability (Thompson 2013).
- Yale University similarly reimagined its introductory physics course for life scientists using examples that emphasized the role

of physical and mathematical concepts in understanding biology, such as force generation by actin polymerization and genetic feedback loops. Student feedback on the new course has been positive, although institutional challenges encountered in developing it included the differing teaching loads of the physics and biology departments, the challenges of adding in a parallel laboratory course, and the issue of adoption by other faculty members and thus course sustainability (Mochrie 2013).

Liberal arts colleges are well known for the numbers of graduates who pursue STEM careers and their general model of education includes science as one dimension of a multidisciplinary curriculum that can align well with the spirit of convergence. Hope College (Michigan), for example, introduces students to interdisciplinary thinking and learning early in their college careers through the use of case studies in all introductory science courses. These cases "focus on compelling, real-world problems, incorporate activities grounded in research on learning, and use a data-rich, research-like approach that develops students' ability to think about problems quantitatively and from different disciplinary perspectives by drawing their attention explicitly to questions of the sources and nature of scientific knowledge" (Hope College 2013). Case studies are used in both laboratory courses as well as in lectures.

Components of a new curriculum can also be designed as modules that can be added and removed with experience and that could be tested during university winter study periods, summer courses, or through seminars. This may be one strategy for testing out-of-the-box approaches to interdisciplinary training, with the expectation that some approaches will fail. A possible model for such modules is the type of specialized short courses taught at the Woods Hole Marine Biological Laboratory or Cold Spring Harbor Laboratory and by universities. In addition to course modules that draw on real problems, challenges such as the International Genetically Engineered Machine (iGEM) competition in synthetic biology can also serve as hooks to promote interest in convergence among students at an early stage of their training.

In graduate student training programs, boot camps, well-crafted journal clubs, seminars, and advanced-level undergraduate gap courses can be useful strategies for enabling students to round out their backgrounds in areas they need to foster convergence. However, failure to receive credit for taking undergraduate courses can create a barrier as graduate students try to complete their coursework and research requirements. To accommodate the need to fill educational gaps, curricular requirements should be flexible within categories. One example of a certificate program that provides grounding in convergent science for graduate students while maintaining disciplinary depth is the Interdisciplinary Quantitative (IQ) Biology Program, established in 2011 at the University of Colorado Bio-Frontiers Institute. Students in the program take a boot camp on computer science, biochemistry, biology, and mathematics as well as a first-year curriculum that integrates quantitative and biological fields before choosing their Ph.D. degree program. The program has also established formal memoranda of understanding (MOUs) with participating academic departments to ensure that the dedicated IQ curriculum does not impede students' timely degree completion (Stith 2013).[3]

For postdoctoral fellows and faculty, short courses and workshops can be tools to foster interdisciplinary training and fill knowledge gaps. So, too, can opportunities such as the Burroughs Wellcome Fund Career Awards at the Scientific Interface[4] or the 2-year Alfred P. Sloan Research Fellowships for early-career scientists. Faculty and postdoctoral fellows can also get involved in co-teaching courses as a strategy to start to learn other disciplines. Summer cross-training opportunities and sabbaticals, as well as seminar-like courses where faculty teach each other, can be other valuable options.

To address additional educational issues related to convergence, one low-cost option is to develop online resources for convergent classes and take advantage of online courses and course modules that a variety of institutions are developing and making available free of charge. Web-based courses can be a tool for filling knowledge gaps, and more research is needed to understand how to make use of them most effectively in combination with person-to-person interactions. Informal learning activities, such as social events and journal clubs, can also be repurposed to address convergence themes.

4.7 CONVERGENCE RELIES ON EFFECTIVE PARTNERSHIP ARRANGEMENTS

Forming effective partnerships is a critical dimension of fostering convergence. As discussed throughout the chapter, many of the connections that underpin convergent activities bridge individual faculty members and academic departments. An additional challenge is posed when par-

---

[3] Federal programs supporting graduate training across disciplinary boundaries included the National Science Foundation's (NSF's) Integrative Graduate Education and Research Traineeship (IGERT), which is currently ending and being replaced with an NSF Research Traineeship program. The IGERT program had a broad mandate across STEM fields and it remains unclear how this may evolve under the new program.

[4] These awards "are targeted toward researchers whose doctoral training is in one of the physical, chemical or computational sciences and who intend to pursue academic research doing work that addresses biological questions" (Burroughs Wellcome Fund 2014).

ticipating investigators and departments cross different schools within an academic institution. The school of arts and science, school of engineering, and school of medicine, for example, may have different policies that govern indirect cost recovery, different expectations for faculty teaching and research loads and salary coverage, or different intellectual property (IP) experiences. Negotiating the numerous MOUs that may be required is time intensive, reaffirming the critical need for committed university leadership.

- *University of Michigan North Campus Research Complex:* In 2008, the University of Michigan purchased Pfizer's former research facility, encompassing 2.2 million square feet of laboratory and administrative space in 28 connected buildings. The university, the medical school, and the university hospital provided money for the purchase and the medical school committed through its department chairs and dean that it would fund the North Campus Research Complex for 10 years with a tax on all incoming grants and income. This money serves as a source of funds for operations and capital improvements so that the campus is not dependent directly on philanthropic funding. However, the medical school had a different model of charging overhead to its faculty that includes capturing depreciation at a significant level as a means of building a fund for new facilities. In contrast, the school of engineering levied no such depreciation charge. This potential roadblock was solved when the university provost created a pool of money to cover the depreciation charge for all nonmedical school faculty. Once the North Campus was created, one of the newly-formed institutes was the Biointerfaces Institute, which explores convergence among nanotechnology, cell and tissue engineering, microfluidics and sensors, and biomaterials and drug delivery. Getting this institute established, however, involved developing an MOU for every single faculty, with every different administrator, in every different department (Canter 2013).

Convergence efforts may also involve partnerships across different universities, as a means to create teams with complementary expertise that may be lacking at any one institution and to enlarge the arena in which researchers can work cooperatively. In the University of California system, the QB3 initiative was established by the State of California to foster convergence between the biological and physical sciences at the universities of Santa Cruz, San Francisco, and Berkeley. One of the strengths of the QB3 collaboration is that the capacities of the three institutions are complementary: Santa Cruz and Berkeley do not have a medical school, while San Francisco does not have an engineering or computer science department. Of the $100 million initially allocated for QB3, one-third went to build a new building on each of the three campuses. However, operating funds dropped almost immediately as a result of state finances. Today, QB3 raises $5 million annually but the University of California chancellors take the majority of those funds, pointing out the potential conflict between those organizing a convergence institute and those whose interests may lie in maintaining separate domains. In a time of limited resources, the competition for funds for both disciplinary and convergent research from development, philanthropy, industry, and government is real and must be accounted for when planning an initiative that spans departments and institutions (Kelly 2013).

Because convergence extends beyond basic science discovery to translational application, bringing clinical, national laboratory, and industry partners into convergent research efforts can provide valuable connections and potentially increase the impact of research. The Ragon Institute, established in 2009 to advance immunology research and vaccine development for diseases such as HIV/AIDS, brings together the clinical expertise of Massachusetts General Hospital with Harvard and MIT. The Institute for Molecular Engineering, established in 2010 as a partnership between the University of Chicago and Argonne National Laboratory, exemplifies a unique relationship in which core faculty hold dual appointments with the university and the national laboratory. The Institute also maintains partnerships with the University of Chicago's Institute for Translational Medicine and the Booth School of Business, which serves as a resource to promote the development of critical entrepreneurship skills (University of Chicago 2014). Finally, industry can be encouraged to join convergence partnerships not only through agreements regarding intellectual property but also by providing access to faculty, ideas, and, perhaps most importantly, students.

As the committee heard repeatedly, developing a well-thought-out MOU that addresses as many contingencies as possible is an important but time-consuming aspect of the process. For the Ragon Institute, for example, structural and financial details about the governance board, institutional operations board, scientific steering committee, intellectual property issues and grant overhead, and mechanisms for inter-institutional collaborations all needed to be spelled out in the MOU (Walker 2013). Collecting and disseminating best practices and model agreements for such MOUs would be useful strategy to enable convergence leaders and practitioners to learn from the experiences of others in the community.

4.8 SUSTAINABLE FUNDING IS NECESSARY
FOR CONVERGENCE EFFORTS

Funding remains a key concern for both individual researchers and institutional leaders engaged in convergence. Federal and nonprofit grant funding is a key source of support for specific convergent research projects, although institutions may catalyze projects through seed funding strategies (see Box 4-3) or may need to find ways to help keep convergent teams together during times when traditional sources of grant funding fall short. Core facilities in life, physical, engineering, and medical sciences needed for convergent research are also expensive and may require dedicated operational staff to maintain these resources and train users. Stable funding for such core facilities can be a particular challenge across the sciences.

For convergent research projects, grant submission and review processes need to fairly account for and evaluate submissions that extend beyond traditional disciplinary boundaries. The creation by funding agencies of transdisciplinary peer-review mechanisms is a positive development that helps to put convergent research on the same footing as more traditional individual investigator-driven research and to facilitate the engagement of researchers in both types of projects. Policy changes at NIH and NSF that allow multiple principal investigators on a grant reflect the kind of cultural change that has been helpful. To further address potential grant issues, the National Cancer Institute (NCI) is creating a

---

BOX 4-3
Seed Funding for Convergence Projects

A crucial role for institutional funding can be in providing seed funds for risky, boundary-pushing convergence projects. As an example of what might be done within an institution to address this challenge, Stanford's Bio-X includes an interdisciplinary initiatives program that provides grants for high-risk research with the potential to transform knowledge. Through an open, university wide competition, the seed grant program provides 20 to 25 awards of about $75,000 a year for 2 years that are designed to be catalytic. Toward that end, the $15 million in seed grants made over the first five rounds of the program have generated over $170 million in follow-on funding (Shatz 2013). The University of Michigan has also instituted a 2-year pilot seed funding program called MCubed. Under the program, each faculty member receives a "token" worth $20,000 but must partner with two other faculty members in order to redeem their tokens for $60,000 of funds and get going on their project idea (Canter 2013).

funding mechanism that enables staff scientists to apply for their own grants rather than as derivatives of a principal investigator's grant. The hope is that this mechanism will improve support for core facilities and infrastructure needed to sustain convergent research activities (D. Singer 2013). At NSF, the Research at the Interface of the Biological, Mathematical, and Physical Sciences (BioMaPS) program aims to foster interactions among research groups in these fields and in engineering to improve understanding of biological systems and to apply that knowledge to areas outside of biomedicine. Other programs at NSF, such as Integrated Support Promoting Interdisciplinary Research and Education (INSPIRE), also represent an effort to support boundary-crossing research and enable program officers rather than peer-review committees to make funding decisions (Roskoski 2013). In an effort to reduce the chances that an innovative idea would be quashed by reviewers without the right balance of expertise, the Department of Energy's Advanced Research Projects Agency-Energy program introduced the concept of a rebuttal phase to its proposal process (Majumdar 2013). It is important to recognize that discipline-based reviewers of grant proposals draw on the depth of their specialized knowledge to make informed judgments about the future prospects of various lines of research. The review process for research proposals at the interfaces of multiple areas of knowledge, such as those arising from convergence, will require the institution of equivalent procedures to critically evaluate the questions and methods proposed.

Another valuable mechanism to support convergence efforts is provided by funding initiatives that support centers. Centers can play an important role in convergence and can act as nucleating agents for a field because without the type of infrastructure that centers build and maintain, it can be hard for a culture of convergence to occur on a sustainable basis. Centers can take different forms, whether as a specific building, a set of core facilities at an institution, or as a funding model. The NIH and NSF both fund relevant center programs, including the Centers in Systems Biology (NIH/National Institute of General Medical Sciences), Centers for Physical Sciences in Oncology (NIH/NCI), or Science and Technology Centers: Integrative Partnerships (NSF).

Foundations are another means of obtaining funding in combination with funds from federal agencies and home institutions (see Box 4-4), although the resources of foundations are much smaller than those of the federal government. For most philanthropic funders, the approach is to be nimble and flexible, and to identify gaps where even a small amount of

BOX 4-4
Convergence Centers Supported by the
Raymond and Beverly Sackler Foundation

Raymond and Beverly Sackler have long sought to invest their philanthropic efforts in the support of basic and applied sciences. Their Foundation, with the guidance and counsel of numerous scientific leaders, has focused on the support of emerging new fields and in the scientists working at those frontiers.

The sequencing of the human genome, advances in regenerative engineering and genetic engineering, and broad advances in the fields of physics, chemistry, and biology have created a myriad of transdisciplinary scientific investigations. The Foundation began over a decade ago to endow programs structured and organized to facilitate scientific investigations now captured under the term "convergence."

To date 12 programs have been funded by the Raymond and Beverly Sackler Foundation with convergence as the guiding principle. These programs, at major academic medical centers and universities in the United States, United Kingdom, and Israel, all enlist cutting-edge leadership and programmatic components. The Foundation felt that its philanthropic support could best be leveraged by allowing flexibility and creativity, and not by imposing a preconceived structure. In effect, each program is a pilot project seeking ways to promote convergence science. An important goal is in supporting a new generation of scientists by creating an optimal research and educational environment that best promotes convergence research.

An example of a Raymond and Beverly Sackler Center is one based at the University of Connecticut under the direction of Dr. Cato T. Laurencin. The Center harnesses the expertise of clinicians, materials scientists, cell and molecular biologists, and engineers with the goal of exploring new approaches toward regenerating tissues. The convergence approach utilized by the Center has helped develop such areas as bioreactor-based musculoskeletal regeneration, and novel uses of nanotechnology to manipulate stem cell response. The Center is a cross-university facility and serves to mentor a broad variety of transdisciplinary scientists.

money can prove valuable.[5] In many instances, foundations also require a financial commitment from the hosting institution.

Many institutions are looking beyond funding agencies and foundations to ensure sustainability of convergence efforts. In addition to endowments, individual donors, venture philanthropy, taxpayer initiatives such as the stem cell bond in California and the Arizona research-targeted sales

---

[5] In 2013, seven foundations announced the formation of a coalition to provide increased funding for basic science research in order to supplement the pivotal support for such research provided by the federal government. The foundations in the coalition include the Howard Hughes Medical Institute, Kavli Foundation, W.M. Keck Foundation, Gordon and Betty Moore Foundation, Research Corporation for Science Advancement, Simons Foundation, and Alfred P. Sloan Foundation.

tax increase, new investment vehicles,[6] and precompetitive partnerships with industry can be sources of long-term funding for convergent research efforts, as well as sources of ideas about mission-critical problems that can attract additional funding sources. The Ragon Institute of Massachusetts General Hospital, MIT, and Harvard, for example, was established though a significant philanthropic donation. However, tapping into these funding opportunities requires that investigators and institute heads understand the needs of diverse funders and how to address those needs. In an era in which government funding is limited, creating the types of partnerships discussed in Section 4.7 may also help leverage federal or state grants to secure additional support from philanthropic or private-sector sources.

4.9 THE CONVERGENCE ECOSYSTEM
INCLUDES CORE ELEMENTS

Many research institutions are engaged in creating an environment that promotes the convergence of life sciences, physical sciences, medicine, engineering, and beyond. Strategies such as organizing space around compelling research themes, providing seed funding to generate preliminary results in high-risk/high-return areas, reforming undergraduate and graduate education, investing in new types of shared and core facilities, recruiting people from industry with expertise in product management and product development, partnering with academic, clinical, and industry collaborators, and exploring multiple sources of funding all contribute to these efforts to nurture an effective convergence ecosystem. Despite differences in size, mission, and organizational structure, the committee identified several common characteristics of successful convergence efforts:

- Committed leaders who are able to communicate a vision, willing to work through potentially contentious and time-consuming issues such as cost sharing, intellectual property ownership, and MOU creation, willing to undertake efforts to raise sustainable funds from multiple sources, and willing to take personal and institutional risks
- Engaged participants at multiple levels who are willing to move beyond intellectual comfort zones, map the scientific landscape, and identify important new challenges to tackle
- A flexible, diverse, and supportive culture

---

[6] For example, the concept of a "megafund" has been proposed as a potential investment mechanism to support early-stage cancer drug development (Fernandez et al. 2012).

- An entrepreneurial spirit in looking for new opportunities at the boundaries and intersections of disciplines that spans basic discovery and translational application
- Partnerships among diverse faculty, among units and schools within a university, and with collaborators such as national laboratories and industry
- Concrete systems for addressing issues such as tenure expectations (for tenure-granting academic organizations) or career tracks and reward structures outside of a tenure framework

Many of the convergence centers of which the committee is aware benefitted significantly from large donors or public taxpayer commitments. Based on many of the examples provided in the report, there may be a concern that only the largest and wealthiest institutions can afford to engage in convergence. But there is undertapped potential in expanding the concept of convergence and the awareness of its benefits to a wider range of institutions—small and large, public and private. As a first step, examples of modest options that could be considered to enable diverse institutions to start to foster convergence are provided in Table 4-2.

TABLE 4-2 Ideas for Fostering Convergence with a Steady State Budget

- Encourage social events such as coffee and pizza to foster presentations and discussions of convergent research.
- Repurpose journal clubs to address convergence themes.
- Foster informal gatherings of faculty with shared interests in convergence problems and topics, which may also contribute to discussions on advancing convergent candidates for faculty positions.
- Establish mechanisms for faculty to hold joint appointments across departments and schools.
- Develop or identify online resources for convergent classes.
- Provide opportunities for experimental courses such as through online tools, collaborative teaching, and teaching "sabbaticals" to develop new courses.
- Include examples in undergraduate and introductory science classes that show how physics, chemistry, math, engineering, and biology are put into practice when dealing with current issues.
- Implement flexible course requirements for graduate students that enable them to fill gaps in knowledge needed to undertake convergent projects and/or the ability for graduate students to name and shape the area of their degree.
- Undertake cluster hires.
- Reduce bureaucratic boundaries.
- Initiate executive-in-residence programs to bring insights from practitioners in industry.
- Institute programs to encourage collaboration at a distance for faculty from different institutions and areas of science.

At the end of the day, modest options alone may not be sufficient to fully implement and sustain a culture of convergence within an institution. Incentives are needed to get and keep people engaged across all levels. These may include funds for research, access to core facilities and to the expertise of others, procedures that reduce or streamline administrative barriers, or the carrot of economic innovation. Generating and sustaining the levels of visibility and enthusiasm needed across the community will require the engagement of key champions within multiple academic institutions, federal agencies, and other partners as well as regular opportunities for stakeholders to share their challenges and map out what is needed to achieve new solutions.

5

Advancing Knowledge and Solving Complex Problems Through Convergence: Conclusions and Recommendations

Convergence builds on advances in life sciences such as understanding the genetic and molecular basis of life. It does so by merging those tools and ways of thinking with contributions from physical sciences, medicine, engineering, and beyond. The promise of accelerated discovery and innovation at these research frontiers, arising from a diversity of perspectives and an environment that embraces those different perspectives, motivates stakeholders across multiple sectors to capitalize on this emerging opportunity.

As the process represented by convergence becomes further embedded in the culture of sciences, the need for institutional structures to support it will grow. Yet, fostering convergence effectively remains a challenge. Convergence institutes are one site for developing new medical therapies, efficient fuels, and improved batteries but other types of institutional settings can also be used to foster convergence. The continued establishment of new convergence centers, such as the recently announced University of Southern California Michelson Center for Convergent Bioscience (Perkins 2014), indicates that practitioner scientists, academic leaders, funders, and collaborative partners share a desire to advance convergent research. This interest underscores the need to capitalize on both existing best practices and new models that will advance this goal.

5.1 CONCLUSIONS AND RECOMMENDATIONS

The committee explored challenges to facilitating convergence, as well as strategies that have been employed by existing convergence programs to address barriers. Based on its analysis of convergence programs established at institutions across the country and the feedback and participation of scientists from graduate students to deans, the committee arrived at the following conclusions and recommendations. While convergence is one of many paths to national scientific and technological leadership, this report documents its emergence as one important mechanism for generating new knowledge, training new students, and contributing to the future of the nation's economy.

> **Conclusion:** *Convergence is a process that leads to significant advances in fundamental knowledge, the creation of new, problem-driven solutions, and strategies for educating the next generation of STEM professionals.*

Discipline-based science has produced a wealth of information across disparate fields. As a result, researchers now have unprecedented opportunities to attack challenging and complex problems. At a time when ideas, methods, models, and intellectual approaches of many fields are being synthesized into an integrated approach to problems of great importance, convergence represents a model that may become increasingly important to scientific discovery and translational application. At the same time, it coexists with many other models of multi- or transdisciplinary approaches, unidisciplinary projects, single–principal investigator (PI) projects, team-based projects, pure basic science, and pure applied science—adding value to the nation's research enterprise. Given this plurality, convergence is one meeting point for many types of complementary initiatives.

> **Conclusion:** *A "one-size-fits-all" approach is not possible when developing an environment that fosters convergence. Differences in institutional size, mission, budgets, and policies impose unique challenges. Nonetheless, essential characteristics of environments supporting convergence can be identified.*

Organizations wishing to establish or enhance a supportive environment for convergence can draw ideas, models, strategies, and lessons from examples at existing institutions in academia, industry, and government. This report has highlighted a variety of such strategies, ranging from journal clubs to innovative building design to the creation of entrepreneurial partnerships that engage stakeholders beyond academia. As the committee's data gathering demonstrated, many methods can foster convergence and the most appropriate approaches differ between institutions. Through comparative analysis, though, the committee was able to articulate essential characteristics of successful convergent ecosystems:

- *People*: The role of leadership committed to supporting convergence is key, as is the distributed leadership of students, faculty, staff, department chairs, and deans at multiple institutional levels. A characteristic of practitioners that facilitates convergence is the ability to communicate across a breadth of areas while building from strong foundations of specific expertise, as represented by the concept of "comb-shaped" individuals.
- *Organization*: As organizations seek ways to build from their established strengths and expand in complementary directions, strategies such as inclusive governance systems, a goal-oriented vision, effective program management, stable support for core facilities, and flexible or catalytic funding sources are fundamental. Because convergence occurs at the intersection of disciplines and the frontiers of knowledge, where risk of failure can be high, organizations must be willing to accept some failures and to phase out or redirect projects that fail.
- *Culture:* The culture needed to support convergence must be inclusive, value diversity of views, and support mutual respect across disciplines. It encourages opportunities to share knowledge and fosters the ability of researchers to be, or to become, conversant across disciplines in bridging knowledge cultures. Interactions across such areas may provide important lessons in building a culture and organization that embodies convergence.
- *Ecosystem*: Many convergence initiatives have spawned local ecosystems in which "technology moves on two feet" (Sharp 2013) as faculty and students engage in research across campus, innovation in nearby startups, and translation with clinical and industry partners.

Conclusion: *If the United States wants to accelerate innovation, building sustainable infrastructure for transdisciplinary cooperation through convergence is a promising strategy. Without a systematic focus, however, even with showcase models, convergence will continue to be a reductive patchwork of isolated efforts.*

Implementing and sustaining the personal, organizational, cultural, and ecosystem-level characteristics necessary to nurture convergence within an organization is a recognized challenge. Bureaucratic overload, disciplinary constraints on faculty hiring and promotion, differences in academic accounting structures, variation in allocation of indirect cost returns, impending changes to the academic health center model that affect research support, and declines of federal research funding are all potential obstacles. Currently, each organization wanting to facilitate convergence develops its own practices to address barriers it encounters. The challenges of convergence, however, mean that institutions must learn from each other in order to expedite the ability of the U.S. research community to harness the potential of convergence.

> **Conclusion:** *Social sciences and humanities scholarship on effectiveness of multi-, inter-, and transdisciplinary teams can inform theory, best practices, and organizational structures employed in convergence programs. Shared practices, especially in areas such as data collection, data access, collaboration, and knowledge dissemination, will also form a strong foundation upon which disparate fields can communicate and converge.*

The evidence of literature reviews, strong models, and the cumulative wisdom of practice affirm that life scientists, physical scientists, and engineers tend to approach problem-solving differently. Challenges at frontiers of disciplines may differ as well. Therefore, case studies of collaborative research efforts, as well as the emergent field of the science of team science, are valuable resources for organizations wishing to optimize structures and practices of convergence programs. The number of convergence organizations already established and the diversity of ages of such programs from the 1990s forward provide a particularly relevant set of case studies that should be investigated more systematically for insights on how to overcome barriers to convergence, what attributes play the most significant roles in nurturing and sustaining convergence, and what types of quantitative and qualitative approaches provide appropriate criteria to evaluate success. Most of the information the committee was able to gather, while useful, was still essentially anecdotal in nature. Moreover, many strategies organizations have used to foster convergence echo the types of challenges and strategies reported for facilitating interdisciplinary and/or team-based research more generally. It would be valuable to examine in more detail the unique barriers to convergence as well as the strategies that have been found to address those challenges successfully. This type of analysis will provide a useful opportunity to further engage the social science research community in helping to answer such questions. While published literature has explored individual case studies and academic-industry center programs such as the National Science

Foundation's (NSF's) Engineering Research Centers, it has not yet focused closely on convergence programs as a group. The results of published studies are challenging to parse for concrete, practical guidance on how to structure a convergence program and establish the necessary policies and agreements. An enhanced and expanded partnership among convergence practitioners, institutional leaders, and the social sciences research community could provide a valuable service in helping to fill this gap.

> **Conclusion:** *Convergence results from merging insights emanating from the integration of diverse perspectives. Further exploration of opportunities will broaden participation in convergence efforts in order to take full advantage of the creativity enabled by diversity of approaches.*

The types of solutions achieved through convergence often arise from teams composed of talented individuals with different backgrounds, experiences, and expertise. Although heterogeneity can lead to conflict as a result of differences in approaches to research problems, diversity also contributes to the power to think beyond usual paradigms and produce creative solutions. Achieving the multiplicative power needed to facilitate convergence involves diversity not only of subject-matter expertise but also of the individual and institutional partners engaged. Most current convergence efforts, particularly established institutes, are associated with a limited number of large, research-intensive universities. To fully take advantage of convergence opportunities, it will be important to continue increasing the range of participants and to harness their insights by creating environments and infrastructures in which multiple talents can be effectively combined.

> **Conclusion:** *Institutional seed funding, catalytic foundation and private funding, and federal agency funding are all constructive mechanisms to support convergence. Federal agencies remain the largest source of academic research and development funding and thus have a special role in facilitating convergence.*

Investigators and institutions use multiple mechanisms to support convergence efforts. All of them are relevant strategies that should continue to be explored, along with alternative strategies such as state bonds or new types of financial instruments such as investment funds. Because federal agencies continue to provide approximately 60 percent of academic research and development funding for science, they are central partners in facilitating convergence. Science agencies have already established programs that recognize and support research at interfaces of multiple disciplines, although the committee was able to identify fewer training grant programs that explicitly address training that spans such boundaries. The National Cancer Institute of the National Institutes of Health (NIH), for example, supports center initiatives such as Transdisciplinary Research on Energetics and Cancer, Centers for Cancer Nanotechnology Excellence, and Physical Sciences in Oncology. The National Institute of Biomedical Imaging and Bioengineering, by the nature of its mandate, brings together expertise from life, physical, and engineering sciences to develop new tools and technologies for clinical innovation. A convergence approach is also embedded in new federal efforts such as Brain Research through Advancing Innovative Neurotechnologies (BRAIN), in which NIH, NSF, and the Defense Advanced Research Projects Agency (DARPA) are partners. Although smaller in scope than federal funding, institutional and foundation funds also play an important role in catalyzing development of convergence projects. Early community discussions to elucidate scientific challenges that ultimately led to the formation of BRAIN were hosted by the Kavli Foundation, for example. These diverse mechanisms for supporting convergence should be maintained and expanded, particularly where support can be leveraged across multiple partners. The NIH Common Fund, in particular, is a promising opportunity for supporting efforts that require convergence approaches. It tackles issues that require strategic planning, coordination, and collaboration across NIH institutes. Similar opportunities and new funding structures at other agencies and across federal science agencies could be explored, such as programs to provide joint funding between agencies.

> **Conclusion:** *The interconnected network of partners, from academic leaders and practitioners to industry researchers, clinicians, and funders, together form an ecosystem for convergence. For convergence to enable innovation and stimulate future economic development and societal problem solving, research advances ultimately need to be translated into new products and services through technology transfer activities such as licensing or the formation of startup companies.*

Problem solving is a key driver for many convergent activities. They have been a fount of new thinking and approaches of the type that have played a significant role in creating disruptive innovations that lead to new job creation. In order to realize a convergence ecosystem, particular attention must be paid to the translational effectiveness of universities. Within U.S. universities, a diverse set of approaches and policies foster commercialization, captured by metrics such as the ratio of federal grants received to number of patents issued or number of companies started. Moreover, effectiveness of universities to license technologies, whether to previously-existing companies or new startup companies, is varied and ranges from effective to ineffective. The federal government makes significant investments in research universities with an implicit expectation that there is return on that public investment. Convergence is a model for how integrated transdisciplinary research can achieve benefits both for the scientific enterprise and for society as advances are translated. For that reason, it is important to evaluate policies and procedures universities use to accomplish the goal of technology translation and how to optimize them.

RECOMMENDATIONS

A series of recommendations follows from these conclusions if the United States wishes to effectively harness the momentum generated by convergence and enable stakeholders to widely foster its further development.

1. **Experts, funding agencies, foundations, and other partners should identify key problems whose solution requires convergence approaches in order to catalyze new research directions and guide research priorities.**
2. **Research institutions, funding agencies, foundations, and other partners should address barriers to effective convergence as they arise, including expanding mechanisms for funding convergence efforts and supporting collaborative proposal review across funding partners. Institutional programs such as seed funding to catalyze collaborations should be implemented or expanded.**
3. **Institutions should review their administrative structures, faculty recruitment and promotion practices, cost recovery models, and research support policies to identify and reduce roadblocks to the formation of inter- and intrainstitutional partnerships that facilitate convergence.**
4. **Academic institutions should develop hiring and promotion policies that include explicit guidelines to recognize the importance of both convergent and disciplinary scholarship, and include criteria to fairly evaluate them.**
5. **Those interested in fostering convergence should identify evidence-based practices that have facilitated convergence by drawing on the expertise of economic, social, and behavioral sciences, as well as program management and strategic planning. Understanding the unique barriers and strategies to practicing convergence would improve practical guidance**

on how institutions can structure and sustain a convergence program.

6. Leaders and practitioners who have fostered a convergence culture in their organizations and laboratories should develop partnerships, synergies, and collaborations with their colleagues—especially in small universities and institutions that serve traditionally underrepresented groups—to help institutions establish and nurture convergence efforts while furthering the interests of their own.

7. Best practices on the effective transfer of technologies from research organizations into the private sector should be collected, established, and disseminated. For convergent approaches to enable innovation and stimulate future economic development, research advances need to be translated into new products and services.

In order to most effectively achieve these goals, the committee concluded that greater coordination will be required to move beyond the patchwork of current efforts. Despite momentum to create and sustain the types of boundary-crossing approaches and partnerships embodied by convergence, fostering convergence successfully remains a challenge. As a result, the committee makes a final recommendation:

8. National coordination on convergence is needed to support the infrastructure to solve emerging problems that transcend traditional boundaries. Stakeholders across the ecosystem of convergence—including agencies, foundations, academic and industry leaders, clinicians, and scientific practitioners—should collaborate to build awareness of the role of convergence in advancing science and technology and stimulating innovation for the benefit of society.

5.2 NATIONAL COORDINATION IS NEEDED

The opportunity for convergence approaches to address challenges of this era—including treating diseases in a precision medicine manner, expanding healthcare access at reduced cost, developing sustainable energy sources, and achieving food and water security—make this the right time for a systematic effort to raise awareness of convergence and its role in sciences and technologies of the future, and to overcome remaining challenges to creating environments that foster it. Over the past several decades, support for cross-disciplinary research has produced a cadre of researchers experienced in convergence approaches. Their readiness, combined with increasingly rapid development of biological understanding and technological progress, presents a new scale of opportunity for convergence. While one-by-one investigator collaborations across disciplines have been productive, we are now witnessing incremental benefits of larger-scale convergence in organizations in measures of research productivity and company establishment.

Institutions, funding agencies, and foundations have all made positive strides in establishing centers of convergence and identifying practices that nurture convergence ecosystems. Nevertheless, many practical challenges identified by convergence leaders and practitioners have remained consistent since release of the 2004 report *Facilitating Interdisciplinary Research* (NAS et al. 2004). Convergence efforts could and should draw in greater numbers of participants from diverse institutions beyond an "elite" tier of large, research-intensive university systems. Convergence is not only transdisciplinary; it is also trans-sector in nature and, like all of science and engineering, international in scope. Although the focus of this committee's data-gathering efforts and the present report is on challenges and strategies for stimulating convergence in U.S. institutions, all areas of science that contribute to convergence are rapidly advancing in a cross-global context. Convergence is a priority for countries participating in EU Research Programmes and in the OECD, thus providing an opportunity for future partnerships. Insight may be gained from learning about practices of convergence centers established elsewhere in the world.

Convergence efforts cross boundaries of life, health, physical, and engineering sciences, and thus also cross boundaries among funding agencies that support biomedical research, such as NIH, and those traditionally supporting research in physical sciences such as the Department of Energy (DOE), NSF, and the Department of Defense (DOD). The power of cross-agency efforts at the interface between life and physical sciences is exemplified by the success of the Human Genome Initiative, which was supported collaboratively by NIH and DOE. Convergent innovation at the edges of disciplines will also be required to help realize the goals of the National Bioeconomy Blueprint. The number of agencies interested in convergence topics represents a powerful base for cross-agency programs.

A systematic focus on convergence would draw attention to available resources in areas such as the science of team science, assessment and evaluation of collaborative research, factors affecting interdisciplinary and transdisciplinary research success, and other areas that bear on the effective implementation of practices that facilitate convergence. Greater coordination on convergence would enable practitioners, funders, and users to learn more about these research fields, which in many cases are drawn from social, economic, and behavioral sciences. The further involvement of faculty from these fields in convergence efforts represents an undertapped resource to aid institutions and investigators as they seek to create environments in their organizations and laboratories that will nurture and sustain convergence. There is clearly community desire for ongoing opportunities to discuss convergence, as exemplified by the dynamic interactions that took place at the 2011 American Association for the Advancement of Science (AAAS)/University of Colorado workshop "Science on FIRE" (Derrick et al. 2012) and the 2013 National Academy of Sciences workshop. Opportunities to continue and deepen these discussions would be beneficial.

Stakeholder discussions on potential convergence challenges would help explore key scientific needs and conceptualize cross-institutional and cross-agency strategies to address them. As noted during the convergence workshop, the White House Office of Science and Technology Policy (OSTP) is an interested consumer of results of processes that can identify challenges and opportunities at the intersection of multiple disciplines; targeted investments needed in research, education, and infrastructure to take advantage of these opportunities; and potential partnerships among agencies, philanthropists, research universities, companies, and other stakeholders that will co-invest in these opportunities (Kalil 2013). Researchers at the interface of neuroscience and nanoscience undertook this type of community planning process when making the case that an investment in new tools was needed to measure real-time activity of neural circuits. This coordinated effort ultimately led to the BRAIN initiative supported by NIH, NSF, and DARPA. The Computing Community Consortium, supported by NSF, similarly issues white papers, research roadmaps, and workshop reports to inform federal research initiatives in areas such as robotics, "big data," and cyberphysical systems. Similar types of efforts to explore the frontiers of convergence would be valuable. At a symposium at the 2014 AAAS annual meeting, participants suggested several health-related topics that require convergence, including developing predictive models for wellness that incorporate new strategies to gather an expanded set of vital signs and understanding and manipulating the microbiome.

As a result, national stakeholder coordination on convergence would support the following five goals:

- Encourage and enable funding agencies and foundations that support research in life, physical, mathematical, computational, medical, and engineering sciences and beyond to support research that spans their established domains and to serve as a network of resources for each other.
- Support the vibrant community of institutional leaders and researchers, both younger and senior, who are interested in fos-

tering convergence and provide an ongoing forum for dialogue among this community on common challenges they encounter and proven strategies used to address them; provide mechanisms to share lessons learned and translate those practices across diverse institutional settings.

- Stimulate further engagement of core partners such as national laboratories, clinicians, industry, and others in the ecosystem of convergence, from discovery to applications; provide opportunities to encourage strategies to simplify funding and simplify administrative structures that govern research between institutions and organizations.

- Draw on experiences of convergence institutes and programs to more systematically understand convergence in institutions and partnering organizations, and to showcase evidence-based practices demonstrated to impact design and conduct of convergent research.

- Catalyze opportunities for the expanding convergence community to discuss frontiers of science and identify emerging topics at interfaces of multiple disciplines where the process of convergence is necessary to achieve new knowledge.

As the examples in the report illustrate, a strong cohort of convergence centers, practitioners, and funders exists as a starting point. This critical mass of activity provides a prime opportunity to sustain and expand convergence discussions. Stakeholders interested in the promise of convergence can help identify scientific research frontiers and help establish priorities. Engagement of communities such as economic, social, and behavioral sciences and humanities can be more effectively incorporated to better understand the process of convergence and to improve translation and adoption of scientific advances that result from convergent research efforts. Diversity of expertise and perspectives is an enabler of innovation and the approach provided by convergence provides one platform to harness such diversity for the benefit of society.

Various models could be considered for how to undertake the national coordination needed to advance convergence. Associations and societies that bring together key stakeholders can undertake convening efforts to set goals. Foundations could serve catalytic roles for the community. Cross-agency working groups could coordinate policy development. All of these actors can play vision-setting roles in the establishment of new strategies to facilitate convergence. At the most structured end is the creation of a formal initiative. Examples of successful initiatives addressing large-scale research problems are well-known, including the Human Genome Project, the Materials Genome Initiative[1], and the recent formation of the BRAIN Initiative. How to establish an initiative around processes and infrastructure, which is what focused coordination on convergence would require, is a more challenging question.

Convergence brings together knowledge and tools from life sciences, physical sciences, medicine, engineering, and beyond in a network of partnerships to undertake innovative research and address compelling technical and societal challenges. It thus has a scope that is diverse, multistakeholder, and multisectorial. One example of an emerging field that is also broad in scope and that engages the contributions of multiple partners is nanoscience. The National Nanotechnology Initiative (NNI) focuses on fostering nanoscience and nanotechnology motivated by the realization that understanding material properties at the nanoscale could have wide-ranging applications across sectors including health, energy, and manufacturing. The NNI provides a framework that brings attention to nanoscience and enables development of shared goals and strategies to advance it. The NNI has catalyzed creation of research and education centers at laboratories and universities across the country, as well as support for public–private partnerships and commercialization activities around nanotechnology. Through the NNI, participating agencies advance fundamental research, stimulate infrastructure, foster workforce education and training, and support grand challenge areas that address compelling priority needs. The NNI currently includes 20 participating agencies with research, regulatory, and commercial missions. It also includes coordinating mechanisms to more effectively leverage the strengths of its diverse participants. The subcommittee on Nanoscale Science, Engineering, and Technology through the National Science and Technology Council at OSTP undertakes strategic planning for this initiative while the National Nanotechnology Coordination Office provides subcommittee support through the organization of meetings, workshops, and the NNI website (www.nano.gov).

To be successful, coordination on convergence will also need to provide a multiagency and multistakeholder framework of shared goals, leverage interests and strengths of research and development agencies such as NIH, NSF, DOE, and DOD and regulatory agencies such as the U.S. Department of Agriculture and the Food and Drug Administration

---

[1] The Materials Genome Initiative, established in 2011, supports research and translation in material science including the development of advanced materials with applications in areas such as energy, transportation, and security (http://www.whitehouse.gov/mgi).

(FDA), foster networks of convergence centers and practitioners in academic, industrial, and clinical settings, and engage the imagination of future convergence scientists. Convergence offers opportunities to build on the success of initiatives such as NNI and others, but the coordination needed by the community to effectively foster convergence focuses even more heavily on processes, mechanisms, partnerships, and infrastructure than on specific technical challenges. One of the goals of national convergence coordination is to better enable stakeholders to identify fruitful research frontiers, which might themselves form the basis for future programs similar to BRAIN.

Convergence among life and health sciences, physical sciences, engineering, and beyond offers the promise of new modes of knowledge creation and production that will stimulate innovation, economic development, and societal problem solving. Many stakeholders in the ecosystem needed for convergence to occur—students and faculty members, academic leaders, practitioners in industry and clinical settings, and representatives of funding agencies, foundations, and the business development community—are already engaged in convergent research and in efforts to nurture it in organizational settings. But challenges remain, including the need to broaden the range of those engaged in convergence efforts. The time is now to bring attention to convergence and to channel that momentum into the practical policies and structures that will enable it to realize its full potential to help transform our world in the 21st century.

References

AAMC and HHMI. (Association of American Medical Colleges and Howard Hughes Medical Institute). 2009. *Scientific Foundations for Future Physicians*. Washington, DC: AAMC [online]. Available: http://www.hhmi.org/sites/default/files/Programs%20and%20Opportunities/aamc-hhmi-2009-report.pdf [accessed February 25, 2014].

American Academy of Arts and Sciences. 2013. *ARISE 2: Unleashing America's Research & Innovation Enterprise*. Cambridge, MA: American Academy of Arts and Sciences [online]. Available: http://www.amacad.org/content/publications/publication.aspx?d=1138 [accessed February 25, 2014].

ARPA-E (The Advanced Research Projects Agency-Energy). 2014. Electrofuels: Microorganisms for Liquid Transportation Fuel. Washington, DC: ARPA-E, U.S. Department of Energy [online]. Available: http://arpa-e.energy.gov/?q=arpa-e-programs/electrofuels [accessed February 27, 2014].

ASU (Arizona State University). 2012. History of Ignite@ ASU [online]. Available: http://community.asu.edu/igniteasu/ [accessed February 27, 2014].

Barker, A. 2013. Key Challenges in the Implementation of Convergence. Presentation to the Workshop Key Challenges in the Implementation of Convergence, National Academy of Sciences, September 16, 2013, Washington, DC.

Becher, T. 1994. The significance of disciplinary differences. *Studies in Higher Education* 19(2):151-161.

Begley, C. G., and L. M. Ellis. 2012. Drug development: Raise standards for preclinical cancer research. *Nature* 483(7391):531-533.

Boardman, C., and B. Bozeman. 2006. Implementing a "bottom-up" multi-sector research collaboration: The case of Texas air quality collaboration. *Economics of Innovation and New Technology* 15(1):51-69.

Boardman, C., and B. Ponomariov. 2014. Management knowledge and the organization of team science in university research centers. *Journal of Technology Transfer* 39(1):75-92.

Boh, W. F., R. Evaristo, and A. Ouderkirk. 2014. Balancing breadth and depth of expertise for innovation: A 3M story. *Research Policy* 43:349-366.

Burroughs Wellcome Fund. 2014. Grant Programs [online]. Available: http://www.bwfund. org/programs-offered [accessed February 28, 2014].

Canter, D. 2013. One Institute's Journey: Vacant to Vibrant. Presentation to the Workshop Key Challenges in the Implementation of Convergence, National Academy of Sciences, September 16, 2013, Washington, DC.

Chang, C. C., E. D. Boland, S. K. Williams, and J. B. Hoying. 2011. Direct-write bioprinting three-dimensional biohybrid systems for future regenerative therapies. *Journal of Biomedical Materials Research, Part B: Applied Biomaterials* 98(1):160-170.

Chrastina, A., K. A. Massey, and J. E. Schnitzer. 2011. Overcoming in vivo barriers to targeted nanodelivery. *Wiley Interdisciplinary Reviews: Nanomedicine and Nanobiotechnology* 3(4):421-437.

Colgoni, A., and C. Eyles. 2010. A new approach to science education for the 21st century. *EDUCAUSE Review* 45(1):10-11 [online]. Available: https://net.educause.edu/ir/library/pdf/ERM1017.pdf [accessed April 9, 2014].

Corley, E. A., P. C. Boardman, and B. Bozeman. 2006. Design and the management of multi-institutional research collaborations: Theoretical implications from two case studies. *Research Policy* 35(7):975-993.

Cummings, J. N., and S. Kiesler. 2005. Collaborative research across disciplinary and organizational boundaries. *Social Studies of Science* 35(5):703-722.

DARPA (Defense Advanced Research Projects Agency). 2014. Open Catalog [online]. Available: http://www.darpa.mil/OpenCatalog/index.html [accessed February 27, 2014].

Derrick, E. G., H. J. Falk-Krzesinski, and M. R. Roberts, eds. 2012. *Facilitating Interdisciplinary Research and Education: A Practical Guide*. Washington, DC: American Association for the Advancement of Science [online]. Available: http://www.aaas.org/report/facilitating-interdisciplinary-research-and-education-practical-guide [accessed February 25, 2014].

Dietz, J. S., and B. Bozeman. 2005. Academic careers, patents, and productivity: Industry experience as scientific and technical human capital. *Research Policy* 34(3):349-367.

Disis, M. L., and J. T. Slattery. 2010. The road we must take: Multidisciplinary team science. *Science Translational Medicine* 2(22):22cm9. Available: http://stm.sciencemag.org/content/2/22/22cm9.full.pdf [accessed April 15, 2014].

Duan, F. and J. C. March. 2010. Engineered bacterial communication prevents *Vibrio cholerae* virulence in an infant mouse model. *Proceedings of the National Academy of Sciences of the United States of America* 107(25):11260-11264.

Dyson, F. 2007. Our biotech future. *The New York Review of Books*, July 19, 2007 [online]. Available: http://www.nybooks.com/articles/archives/2007/jul/19/our-biotech-future/?pagination=false [accessed February 26, 2014].

Elrod, S., and M. J. S. Roth. 2012. *Leadership for Interdisciplinary Learning: A Practical Guide to Mobilizing, Implementing, and Sustaining Campus Efforts*. Washington, DC: Association of American Colleges and Universities.

Ely, R. J., and D. A. Thomas. 2001. Cultural diversity at work: The effects of diversity perspectives on work group processes and outcomes. *Administrative Science Quarterly* 46(2): 229-273.

ERC (Engineering Research Centers). 2014. *Best Practice Manual* [online]. Available: http://erc-assoc.org/best_practices/best-practices-manual [accessed February 27, 2014].

Fernandez, J. M., R. M. Stein, and A. W. Lo. 2012. Commercializing biomedical research through securitization techniques. *Nature Biotechnology* 30(10):964-975.

Ferris, C. J., K. G. Gilmore, G. G. Wallace, and M. In het Panhuis. 2013. Biofabrication: An overview of the approaches used for printing of living cells. *Applied Microbiology and Biotechnology* 97(10):4243-4258.

Fountain, H. 2013. At the Printer, Living Tissue. *New York Times*, August 18 [online]. Available: http://www.nytimes.com/2013/08/20/science/next-out-of-the-printer-living-tissue.html?_r=0 [accessed February 26, 2014].

Georgia Tech. 2014. Parker H. Petit Institute for Bioengineering and Bioscience [online]. Available: http://www.ibb.gatech.edu/ [accessed February 28, 2014].

Gross, B. C., J. L. Erkal, S. Y. Lockwood, C. Chen, and D. M. Spence. 2014. Evaluation of 3D printing and its potential impact on biotechnology and the chemical sciences. *Analytical Chemistry* [online]. Available: http://pubs.acs.org/doi/pdf/10.1021/ac403397r [accessed February 26, 2014].

Guest, D. 1991. The hunt is on for the Renaissance Man of computing. *The Independent (London)*, September 17.

Guillotin, B., and F. Guillemot. 2011. Cell patterning technologies for organotypic tissue fabrication. *Trends in Biotechnology* 29(4):183-190.

Hall, K. L. 2013. Recognition for Team Science and Cross-disciplinarity in Academia: An Exploration of Promotion and Tenure Policy and Guideline Language from Clinical and Translational Science Awards (CTSA) Institutions. Presentation at the National Academies Workshop on Institutional and Organizational Supports for Team Science, October 24, 2013, Washington, DC.

Hall, K. L., D. Stokols, R. P. Moser, B. K. Taylor, M. D. Thornquist, L. C. Nebeling, C. C.Ehret, M. J. Barnett, A. McTiernan, N. A. Berger, M. I. Goran, and R. W. Jeffery. 2008. The collaboration readiness of transdisciplinary research teams and centers: Findings from the National Cancer Institute's TREC year-one evaluation study. *American Journal of Preventive Medicine* 35(2S):S161-S172.

Hall, K. L., D. Stokols, B. A. Stipelman, A. L. Vogel, A. Feng, B. Masimore, G. Morgan, R. P. Moser, S. E. Marcus, and D. Berrigan. 2012. Assessing the value of team science: A study comparing center- and investigator-initiated grants. *American Journal of Preventive Medicine* 42(2):157-163.

Hollingsworth, J. R. 2002. Research Organizations and Major Discoveries in Twentieth-Century Science: A Case Study of Excellence in Biomedical Research. Discussion Paper No. P 02-003. *Wissenschaftszentrum Berlin für Sozialforschung* [online]. Available: http://econstor.eu/bitstream/10419/50229/1/360099068.pdf [accessed March 4, 2014].

Hong, L., and S. E. Page. 2004. Groups of diverse problem solvers can outperform groups of high-ability problem solvers. *Proceedings of the National Academy of Sciences of the United States of America* 101(46):16385-16389.

Hope College. 2013. Interdisciplinary Case Studies. Howard Hughes Medical Institute [online]. Available: http://www.hope.edu/academic/hhmi/curriculum/interdisciplinary%20case%20studies.html

Horowitz, S. K. and I. B. Horowitz. 2007. The effects of team diversity on team outcomes: A meta-analytic review of team demography. *Journal of Management* 33(6):987-1015.

Illumina. 2014. History of Illumina Sequencing. Illumina, Inc., San Diego, CA [online]. Available: http://www.illumina.com/technology/solexa_technology.ilmn [accessed April 29, 2014].

Ingber, D. 2013. Wyss Institute: A New Model for Innovation, Collaboration and Technology Translation. Presentation to the Workshop Key Challenges in the Implementation of Convergence, National Academy of Sciences, September 16, 2013, Washington, DC.

IOP (Institute of Physics). 2009. Physics for an Advanced World. London: IOP [online]. Available: http://www.iop.org/publications/iop/2009/file_38209.pdf [accessed February 25, 2014].

Jacks, T. 2013. Convergence, Cancer Research and the Koch Institute Experience at MIT. Presentation to the Workshop on Science Team Dynamics and Effectiveness, July 1, 2013, Washington, DC [online]. Available: http://www.tvworldwide.com/events/nas/130701/ [accessed February 28, 2014].

Jacobs, J. A. 2013. *In Defense of Disciplines: Interdisciplinarity and Specialization in the Research University*. University of Chicago Press.

Jain, K. K. 2012. Nanobiotechnology-based strategies for crossing the blood-brain barrier. *Nanomedicine* 7(8):1225-1233.

Kabo, F., Y. Hwang, M. Levenstein, and J. Owen-Smith. 2013. Shared paths to the lab: A Sociospatial Network Analysis of Collaboration. *Environment and Behavior* [online]. Available: http://eab.sagepub.com/content/early/2013/07/20/0013916513493909. abstract [accessed February 26, 2014].

Kalil, T. 2013. How the Goals of Convergence Complement OSTP Priorities and Activities. Remarks to the Workshop Key Challenges in the Implementation of Convergence, National Academy of Sciences, September 16, 2013, Washington, DC.

Kelly, R. 2013. Inter-institutional Arrangements and Partnerships. Presentation to the Workshop Key Challenges in the Implementation of Convergence, National Academy of Sciences, September 16, 2013, Washington, DC.

Khripin, C. Y., D. Pristinski, D.R. Dunphy, C.J. Brinker, and B. Kaehr. 2011. Protein-directed assembly of arbitrary three-dimensional nanoporous silica architectures. *ACS Nano* 5:1401-1409.

Klein, J. T. 2010a. A taxonomy of interdisciplinarity. Pp. 15-30 in *Oxford Handbook of Interdisciplinarity*, edited by R. Frodeman, J. T. Klein, and C. Mitcham. Oxford: Oxford University Press.

Klein, J. T. 2010b. *Creating Interdisciplinary Campus Cultures: A Model for Strength and Sustainability*. San Francisco, CA: Jossey-Bass.

Koch, L., M. Gruene, C. Unger, and B. Chichkov. 2013. Laser assisted cell printing. *Current Pharmaceutical Biotechnology* 14(1):91-97.

Lewis, J. M., S. Ross, and T. Holden. 2012. The how and why of academic collaboration: Disciplinary differences and policy implications. *Higher Education* 64(5):693-708.

Lucibella, M. 2012. Deconstructing the iPad: How federally supported research leads to game-changing innovation. *APS Physics Frontline* [online]. Available: http://physicsfrontline.aps.org/2012/04/02/deconstructing-the-ipad-how-federally-funded-supported-research-leads-to-game-changing-innovation-2/ [accessed February 25, 2014].

Luo, W., X. Wang, C. Meyers, N. Wannenmacher, W. Sirisaksoontorn, M. M. Lerner, and X. Ji. 2013. Efficient fabrication of nanoporous Si and Si/Ge enabled by the heat scavenger in magnesiothermic reactions. *Scientific Reports* 3:Art.2222.

Majumdar, A. 2013. Challenges of Convergent Thinking and Innovation. Presentation to the Workshop Key Challenges in the Implementation of Convergence, National Academy of Sciences, September 16, 2013, Washington, DC.

Martinez, F. 2013. Faculty Issues: A Matter of Leadership and Governance. Presentation to the Workshop Key Challenges in the Implementation of Convergence, National Academy of Sciences, September 16, 2013, Washington, DC.

Mayo Clinic. 2013. 3D Printer Uses CT Scan to Print out Model of Hip Joint Before Surgery. Mayo Clinic News Network Press Release: April 10, 2013 [online]. Available: http://newsnetwork.mayoclinic.org/discussion/3d-printer-uses-ct-scan-to-print-out-model-of-hip-joint-before-surgery [accessed February 26, 2014].

Mochrie, S. 2013. PHYS 170: Introductory Physics for Life Scientists Reimagined. Presentation to the Workshop Key Challenges in the Implementation of Convergence, National Academy of Sciences, September 16, 2013, Washington, DC.

NAS, NAE, and IOM (National Academy of Sciences, National Academy of Engineering, and Institute of Medicine). 2004. *Facilitating Interdisciplinary Research*. Washington, DC: The National Academies Press.

NAS, NAE, and IOM. 2013. Keck Futures Initiative [online]. Available: http://www.keckfutures.org/ [accessed February 26, 2014].

NCSE (National Council for Science and Environment). 2014. Interdisciplinary Tenure and Career Development Committee [online]. Available: http://ncseonline.org/programs/ education-careers/cedd/projects/faculty-development# [accessed February 27, 2014].

NCI (National Cancer institute). 2014. Team Science Toolkit [online]. Available: https:// www.teamsciencetoolkit.cancer.gov/public/Home.aspx [accessed February 27, 2014].

NNI (National Nanotechnology Initiative). 2014. Nanotechnology [online]. Available: http://www.nano.gov [accessed February 26, 2014].

Nooteboom, B., W. Van Haverbeke, G. Duysters, V. Gilsing, and A. van den Oord. 2007. Optimal cognitive distance and absorptive capacity. *Research Policy* 36(7):1016-1034.

NRC (National Research Council). 2003. *BIO2010: Transforming Undergraduate Education for Future Research Biologists.* Washington, DC: The National Academies Press.

NRC. 2005a. *Mathematics and 21st Century Biology.* Washington, DC: The National Academies Press.

NRC. 2005b. *Catalyzing Inquiry at the Interface of Computing and Biology.* Washington, DC: The National Academies Press.

NRC. 2007. *Rising Above the Gathering Storm: Energizing and Employing America for a Brighter Economic Future.* Washington, DC: The National Academies Press.

NRC. 2008. *Inspired by Biology: From Molecules to Materials to Machines.* Washington, DC: The National Academies Press.

NRC. 2009. *A New Biology for the 21st Century.* Washington, DC: The National Academies Press.

NRC. 2010. *Research at the Intersection of the Physical and Life Sciences.* Washington, DC: The National Academies Press.

NRC. 2011a. *Toward Precision Medicine: Building a Knowledge Network for Biomedical Research and a New Taxonomy of Disease.* Washington, DC: The National Academies Press.

NRC. 2011b. *Research Training in the Biomedical, Behavioral, and Clinical Research Sciences.* Washington, DC: The National Academies Press.

NRC. 2011c. *A Data-Based Assessment of Research-Doctorate Programs in the United States.* Washington, DC: The National Academies Press.

NRC. 2011d. *Life Sciences and Related Fields: Trends Relevant to the Biological Weapons Convention.* Washington, DC: The National Academies Press.

NRC. 2012a. *Research Universities and the Future of America: Ten Breakthrough Actions Vital to Our Nation's Prosperity and Security.* Washington, DC: The National Academies Press.

NRC. 2012b. *Research Frontiers in Bioinspired Energy: Molecular-Level Learning from Natural Systems: A Workshop.* Washington, DC: The National Academies Press.

NRC. 2012c. *Discipline-Based Education Research: Understanding and Improving Learning in Undergraduate Science and Engineering.* Washington, DC: The National Academies Press.

NRC. 2012d. *Challenges in Chemistry Graduate Education: A Workshop Summary.* Washington, DC: The National Academies Press.

NRC. 2013. *Education for Life and Work: Developing Transferable Knowledge and Skills in the 21st Century.* Washington, DC: The National Academies Press.

NRC. 2014. Project: The Science of Team Science [online]. Available: http://sites.nation-alacademies.org/dbasse/bbcss/currentprojects/dbasse_080231 [accessed February 27, 2014].

NSF (National Science Foundation). 2012. Academic research and development. Chapter 5 in *Science and Engineering Indicators 2012.* Arlington, VA: NSF [online]. Available: http:// www.nsf.gov/statistics/seind12/pdf/c05.pdf [accessed February 25, 2014].

NSF. 2014. Academic research and development. Chapter 5 in *Science and Engineering Indicators 2014.* Arlington, VA: NSF [online]. Available: http://www.nsf.gov/statistics/ seind14/content/chapter-5/chapter-5.pdf [accessed March 10, 2014].

Organovo. 2014. The Bioprinting Process. Organovo Holdings, Inc., San Diego, CA [online]. Available: http://www.organovo.com/science-technology/bioprinting-process [accessed February 26, 2014].

Ozbolat, I.T., and Y. Yu. 2013. Bioprinting toward organ fabrication: Challenges and future trends. *Transactions on Biomedical Engineering* 60(3):691-699.

Patel, M., E. B. Souto, and K. K. Singh. 2013. Advances in brain drug targeting and delivery: Limitations and challenges of solid lipid nanoparticles. *Expert Opinion on Drug Delivery* 10(7):889-905.

PCAST (President's Council of Advisors on Science and Technology). 2012. *Engage to Excel: Producing One Million Additional College Graduates with Degrees in Science, Technology, Engineering, and Mathematics* [online]. Available: http://www.whitehouse.gov/sites/default/files/microsites/ostp/pcast-executive-report-final_2-13-12.pdf [accessed February 25, 2014].

Perkins, R. 2014. $50 Million Gift Funds Convergent Bioscience Research at USC. University of Southern California News [online]. Available: http://news.usc.edu/#!/article/58206/michelson/ [accessed February 28, 2014].

Pescosolido, B. A., Martin, J. K., McLeod, J. D., and A. Rogers, eds. 2012. *The Handbook of Sociology of Health, Illness and Healing: A Blueprint for the 21st Century*. New York: Springer.

Pollack, M. E., and M. Snir. 2008. Promotion and Tenure of Interdisciplinary Faculty. Best Practice Memo: September 2008. The Computing Research Association [online]. Available: http://cra.org/resources/bp-view/best_practices_memo_promotion_and_tenure_of_interdisciplinary_faculty/ [accessed February 27, 2014].

Porter, A. L., and I. Rafols. 2009. Is science becoming more interdisciplinary? Measuring and mapping six research fields over time. *Scientometrics* 81(3):719-745.

Porter, A. L., J. D. Roessner, and A. E. Heberger. 2008. How interdisciplinary is a given body of research? *Research Evaluation* 17(4):273-282.

Princeton University. 2013. The Lewis-Sigler Institute for Integrative Genomics [online]. Available: http://www.princeton.edu/genomics/ [accessed February 27, 2014].

Prinz, F., T. Schlange, and K. Asadullah. 2011. Believe it or not: How much can we rely on published data on potential drug targets? *Nature Reviews Drug Discovery* 10(9):712.

Ritter, S. K. 2011. Electrofuels bump up solar efficiency. *Chemical & Engineering News* 89(48): 36-37.

Roco, M. C., W. S. Bainbridge, B. Tonn, and G. Whitesides, eds. 2013. *Convergence of Knowledge, Technology, and Society: Beyond Convergence of Nano-Bio-Info-Cognitive Technologies*. New York: Springer.

Roskoski, J. 2013. Funding Models. Remarks and Panel Discussion to the Workshop Key Challenges in the Implementation of Convergence, National Academy of Sciences, September 17, 2013, Washington, DC.

Rubin, G. 2013. Faculty Issue. Presentation to the Workshop Key Challenges in the Implementation of Convergence, National Academy of Sciences, September 16, 2013, Washington, DC.

Science. 2013. Grand Challenges in Science Education. Science Special Issue: April 19.

Sharp, P. 2013. Presentation to the Workshop Key Challenges in the Implementation of Convergence, National Academy of Sciences, September 16, 2013, Washington, DC.

Sharp, P. A., and R. Langer. 2011. Promoting convergence in biomedical science. *Science* 333(6042):527.

Sharp, P. A., and R. Langer. 2013. Convergence of engineering and life sciences [editorial]. *The Bridge* 43(3): 3-6.

Sharp. P. A., and A. I. Leshner. 2014. Meeting global challenges [editorial]. *Science* 343(6171): 579.

Sharp, P. A., C. L. Cooney, M. A. Kastner, J. Lees, R. Sasisekharan, M. B. Yaffe, S. N. Bhatia, T. E. Jacks, D. A. Lauffenburger, R. Langer, P. T. Hammond, and M. Sur. 2011. *The Third Revolution: The Convergence of the Life Sciences, Physical Sciences, and Engineering.* Washington, DC: Massachusetts Institute of Technology [online]. Available: http://dc.mit.edu/sites/dc.mit.edu/files/MIT%20White%20Paper%20on%20Convergence.pdf [accessed February 26, 2014].

Shatz, C. 2013. The X in Stanford Bio-X. Presentation to the Workshop Key Challenges in the Implementation of Convergence, National Academy of Sciences, September 16, 2013, Washington DC.

Singer, D. 2013. Funding Models. Remarks and Panel Discussion to the Workshop Key Challenges in the Implementation of Convergence, National Academy of Sciences, September 17, 2013, Washington, DC.

Singer, S. 2013. Convergence at Liberal Arts Colleges. Presentation to the Workshop Key Challenges in the Implementation of Convergence, National Academy of Sciences, September 16, 2013, Washington, DC.

Stith, A. 2013. Education and Training: IQ Biology PhD Certificate Program. Presentation to the Workshop Key Challenges in the Implementation of Convergence, National Academy of Sciences, September 16, 2013, Washington, DC.

Stahl, G. K., M. L. Maznevski, A. Voigt, and K. Jonsen. 2010. Unraveling the effects of cultural diversity in teams: A meta-analysis of multicultural work groups. *Journal of International Business Studies* 41: 690-709.

Stokols, D., S. Misra, R. P. Moser, K. L. Hall, and B. K. Taylor. 2008. The ecology of team science: Understanding contextual influences on transdisciplinary collaboration. *American Journal of Preventive Medicine* 35(2S):S96-S115.

Thompson, K. 2013. Facilitating Convergence in Undergraduate Biology Curricula. Presentation to the Workshop Key Challenges in the Implementation of Convergence, National Academy of Sciences, September 16, 2013, Washington, DC.

Toker, U., and D. O. Gray. 2008. Innovation spaces: Workspace planning and innovation in U.S. university research centers. *Research Policy* 37:309–329.

Tosi, G., B. Bortot, B. Ruozi, D. Dolcetta, M. A. Vandelli, F. Forni, and G. M. Severini. 2013. Potential use of polymeric nanoparticles for drug delivery across the blood-brain barrier. *Current Medicinal Chemistry* 20(17):2212-2225.

University of Chicago. 2014. Institute for Molecular Engineering: Research Themes [online]. Available: http://ime.uchicago.edu/ [accessed February 27, 2014].

University of Colorado. 2014. BioFrontiers Institute [online]. Available: http://biofrontiers.colorado.edu/ [accessed February 27, 2014].

University of Iowa. 2014. Cluster Hiring Initiative [online]. Available: http://provost.uiowa.edu/cluster-hire-initiative [accessed February 27, 2014].

University of Missouri. 2014. Cristopher Bond Life Science Center [online]. Available: http://bondlsc.missouri.edu/ [accessed February 27, 2014].

University of Pennsylvania. 2014. Penn Nano Cluster-Hiring Initiative [online]. Available: http://www.nano.upenn.edu/about/hiring-initiative/ [accessed February 27, 2014].

University of Wisconsin-Madison. 2014a. Cluster Hiring Initiative [online]. Available: http://clusters.wisc.edu/index.htm [accessed February 27, 2014].

University of Wisconsin-Madison. 2014b. Wisconsin Institute for Discovery: Interior Features [online]. Available: https://discovery.wisc.edu/home/discovery/facility/interior-features/ [accessed February 28, 2014].

Urban, R., and P. Grodzinski. 2013. Implications: Human health and physical potential. Pp. 171-200 in *Convergence of Knowledge, Technology, and Society: Beyond Convergence of Nano-Bio-Info-Cognitive Technologies,* edited by M. C. Roco, W. S. Bainbridge, B. Tonn, and G. Whitesides. New York: Springer.

USC (University of South California). 2013. UCAPT Manual, March 2013. University Committee on Appointments, Promotions and Tenure [online]. Available: http://policies. usc.edu/p4acad_stud/appointments_promotion_tenure.pdf [accessed February 27, 2014].

Venter, C., and D. Cohen. 2004. The century of biology. *New Perspectives Quarterly* 21(4):73-77.

Vrieling, E. G., Q. Sun, T. P. Beelen, S. Hazelaar, W. W. Gieskes, R. A. van Santen, and N. A. Sommerdijk. 2005. Controlled silica synthesis inspired by diatom silicon biomineralization. *Journal of Nanoscience and Nanotechnology* 5(1):68-78.

Wagner, C. S., J. D. Roessner, K. Bobb, J. T. Klein, K. W. Boyack, J. Keyton, I. Rafols, and K. Borner. 2011. Approaches to understanding and measuring interdisciplinary scientific research (IDR): A review of the literature. *Journal of Informetrics* 165(1):14-26.

Walker, B. 2013. Implementation of Convergence: A Case Study. Presentation to the Workshop Key Challenges in the Implementation of Convergence, National Academy of Sciences, September 16, 2013, Washington, DC.

Wendler, C., B. Bridgeman, F. Cline, C. Millett, J. Rock, N. Bell, and P. McAllister. 2010. *The Path Forward: The Future of Graduate Education in the United States.* Princeton, NJ: *Educational Testing Service* [online]. Available: http://www.fgereport.org/rsc/pdf/ CFGE_report.pdf [accessed February 26, 2014].

Wendler, C., B. Bridgeman, R. Markle, F. Cline, N. Bell, P. McAllister, and J. Kent. 2012. *Pathways Through Graduate School and Into Careers. Princeton, NJ: Educational Testing Service* [online]. Available: http://pathwaysreport.org/rsc/pdf/19089_PathwaysRept_Links. pdf [accessed February 26, 2014].

White House. 2012. *National Bioeconomy Blueprint* [online]. Available: http://www.white house.gov/sites/default/files/microsites/ostp/national_bioeconomy_blueprint_ april_2012.pdf [accessed February 27, 2014].

Zinner, D. E., and E. G. Campbell. 2009. Life-science research within U.S. academic medical centers. *Journal of the American Medical Association* 302(9):969-976. JAMA 302(9):969-976.

A

Committee Member Biographies

Joseph M. DeSimone is Chancellor's Eminent Professor of Chemistry at the University of North Carolina at Chapel Hill (UNC) and William R. Kenan Jr. Professor of Chemical Engineering at North Carolina State University. He is also the director of the Frank Hawkins Kenan Institute of Private Enterprise at UNC and is an adjunct member at Memorial Sloan-Kettering Cancer Center in New York. His interests include applying lithographic techniques from the computer industry to the design of new medicines and vaccines; colloid, surfactant and surface chemistry; the role of diversity in innovation; and entrepreneurship from research-intensive universities. Dr. DeSimone has published over 290 scientific articles and has more than 130 issued patents in his name. In 2004 Dr. DeSimone launched Liquidia Technologies, which now employs roughly 50 people and has raised over $60 million in venture financing, including the first ever equity investment by the Bill & Melinda Gates Foundation in a for-profit biotech company. Liquidia has converted a soft lithography method, PRINT, into a GMP-compliant process and has recently brought its first product, a seasonal influenza vaccine based on PRINT particles, into its first clinical trial. Dr. DeSimone received his B.S. in chemistry in 1986 from Ursinus College in Collegeville, Pennsylvania and his Ph.D. in chemistry in 1990 from Virginia Tech. He is a member of the National Academy of Sciences and the National Academy of Engineering.

Timothy Galitski is an affiliate professor at the Institute for Systems Biology (ISB) in Seattle, and recently Head of Science & Technology in the

Bioscience Business Unit of EMD Millipore Corporation. Previously at the ISB for 10 years, he was a professor and a member of the leadership team that grew the institution from a handful of employees to a transformational organization with global scientific impact. His education, training, and research span the fields of genetics, microbiology, molecular and cell biology, functional genomics, proteomics, microfluidics technology development, and computational biology. Dr. Galitski earned his Ph.D. in the University of Utah's Department of Biology where he identified mechanisms of chromosome rearrangement and studied the origin of genetic variation. His research earned him the 1996 James W. Prahl Memorial Award for the Outstanding Graduate Student at the University of Utah Medical Center. With a fellowship from the Helen Hay Whitney Foundation, Dr. Galitski went on to a postdoctoral position at the Whitehead Institute for Biomedical Research and the Whitehead/MIT Center for Genome Research in Cambridge, Massachusetts. There he combined functional genomics, genetics, and computational methods to reveal global patterns of gene expression specifying cell type and developmental potential in yeast. For this work, Dr. Galitski was awarded the 2001 Burroughs Wellcome Fund Career Award in the Biomedical Sciences.

James M. Gentile is dean of the division of Natural and Applied Sciences at Hope College in Holland, Michigan. He is the former president of Research Corporation for Science Advancement, a foundation dedicated to science since 1912 and the second-oldest foundation in the United States (after the Carnegie Corporation). A geneticist by training, Dr. Gentile has conducted extensive research on the role of metabolism in the conversion of natural and xenobiotic agents into mutagens and carcinogens, with funding from the National Institutes of Health, the National Science Foundation, the U.S. Environmental Protection Agency, and the World Health Organization, among many other institutions. He received his doctorate from Illinois State University and spent 2 years in postdoctoral studies in the Department of Human Genetics at the Yale University School of Medicine. He is the author of more than 150 research articles, book chapters, book reviews, and special reports in areas of scientific research and higher education, and he is a frequent speaker on issues involving the integration of scientific research and higher education.

Sharon C. Glotzer is the Stuart W. Churchill Collegiate Professor of Chemical Engineering and Professor of Materials Science and Engineering at the University of Michigan, Ann Arbor. She also holds faculty appointments in Physics, Applied Physics, and Macromolecular Science and Engineering. Dr. Glotzer's research focuses on computational nanoscience and simulation of soft matter, self-assembly, and materials design, and is sponsored by the U.S. Department of Defense, U.S. Department of Energy, U.S. National Science Foundation, the J.S. McDonnell Foundation, and the Simons Foundation. Sharon C. Glotzer is an internationally recognized scientist, with over 170 publications and over 260 invited, keynote, and plenary talks on five continents. In addition to numerous awards and honors, Dr. Glotzer was elected in 2011 to the American Academy of Arts and Sciences, is a Fellow of the American Physical Society (APS) and a National Security Science and Engineering Faculty Fellow, and was named a Simons Investigator in 2012, the inaugural year of that program. Dr. Glotzer serves on many editorial and advisory boards and has provided leadership and input on roadmapping for federal granting agencies on many topics, including high-performance computing, materials design, technology warning, and simulation-based engineering and science.

Susan Hockfield is professor of neuroscience at the Massachusetts Institute of Technology (MIT) and served as the 16th president of MIT from December 2004 through June 2012. After earning a B.A. in biology from the University of Rochester and a Ph.D. from the Georgetown University School of Medicine, Dr. Hockfield was an NIH postdoctoral fellow at the University of California, San Francisco. She then joined the scientific staff at the Cold Spring Harbor Laboratory in New York. Joining the faculty of Yale University in 1985, Dr. Hockfield focused her research on the development of the brain and on glioma, a deadly form of brain cancer, and pioneered the use of monoclonal antibody technology in brain research. She gained tenure in 1994 and was later named the William Edward Gilbert Professor of Neurobiology. She served as dean of Yale's Graduate School of Arts and Sciences and then as provost. Dr. Hockfield holds honorary degrees from institutions including Brown University, Mt. Sinai School of Medicine, Tsinghua University (Beijing), University of Edinburgh, Université Pierre et Marie Curie, University of Massachusetts Medical School, University of Rochester, and the Watson School of Biological Sciences at the Cold Spring Harbor Laboratory. Her accomplishments have been recognized by the Charles Judson Herrick Award from the American Association of Anatomists, the Wilbur Lucius Cross Award from the Yale University Graduate School, the Meliora Citation from the University of Rochester, the Golden Plate Award from the Academy of Achievement, the Amelia Earhart Award from the Women's Union, the Edison Award, and the Pinnacle Award for Lifetime Achievement from the Greater Boston Chamber of Commerce.

Julie Thompson Klein is professor of humanities in the English Department and Faculty Fellow for Interdisciplinary Development in the Division of Research at Wayne State University. Holder of a Ph.D. in English from the University of Oregon, Dr. Klein is past president of the Association for Integrative Studies (AIS) and former editor of the AIS journal *Issues in Integrative Studies.* Her books include *Interdisciplinarity: History, Theory, and Practice* (1990), *Interdisciplinary Studies Today* (coedited, 1994), *Crossing Boundaries: Knowledge, Disciplinarities, and Interdisciplinarities* (1996), *Transdisciplinarity: Joint Problem Solving among Science, Technology, and Society* (coedited, 2001), *Interdisciplinary Education in K-l2 and College* (edited, 2002), the monograph *Mapping Interdisciplinary Studies* (1999), *Humanities, Culture, and Interdisciplinarity: The Changing American Academy* (2005), and *Creating Interdisciplinary Campus Cultures* (2010). She was also Associate Editor of the *Oxford Handbook on Interdisciplinarity* (2010), and author of numerous chapters and articles. Dr. Klein was elected to the Wayne State University Academy of Scholars and is a recipient of the President's Award for Excellence in Teaching, the Graduate Mentor Award, the Board of Governors Distinguished Faculty Award, and Board of Governors Distinguished Faculty Fellowship. She won the final prize in the Van Eesteren-Fluck & Van Lohuizen Foundation's international competition for new research models and has received the Kenneth Boulding Award for outstanding scholarship on interdisciplinarity, the Yamamoorthy and Yeh Distinguished Transdisciplinary Achievement Award, and the Joseph Katz Award for Distinguished Contributions to the Practice and Discourse of General and Liberal Education. She was also senior fellow at the Association of American Colleges and Universities (AACU) in 1997-98, was appointed continuing senior fellow at the University of North Texas Center for the Study of Interdisciplinarity in 2009, in Fall 2008 was an invited visiting fellow at the University of Michigan's Institute for the Humanities, and in Fall 2011 was Mellon Fellow and Visiting Professor in Digital Humanities.

Cato T. Laurencin is a designated University Professor at the University of Connecticut and the Albert and Wilda Van Dusen Distinguished Endowed Professor of Orthopaedic Surgery and Professor of Chemical Engineering, Materials Engineering and Biomedical Engineering at the school. An internationally prominent orthopedic surgeon, engineer, and administrator, Dr. Laurencin is the founder and director of both the Institute for Regenerative Engineering and the Raymond and Beverly Sackler Center for Biomedical, Biological, Physical and Engineering Sciences at the University of Connecticut Health Center. In addition, he serves as the chief executive officer of the Connecticut Institute for Clinical and Translational Science at the University of Connecticut. Dr. Laurencin has been a member of the National Science Foundation's Advisory Committee for Engineering (ADCOM) and has served both on the National Science Board of the FDA and the National Advisory Council for Arthritis, Musculoskeletal and Skin Diseases at the National Institutes of Health (NIH). He is currently a member of the National Advisory Council for Biomedical Imaging and Bioengineering and the Advisory Committee to the NIH Director. Dr. Laurencin earned his undergraduate degree in chemical engineering from Princeton University and his medical degree magna cum laude from Harvard Medical School. During medical school, he also earned his Ph.D. in biochemical engineering/biotechnology from the Massachusetts Institute of Technology. He is an elected member of the Institute of Medicine and the National Academy of Engineering.

Cherry A. Murray is dean of Harvard University's School of Engineering and Applied Sciences, John A. and Elizabeth S. Armstrong Professor of Engineering and Applied Sciences, and professor of physics. Previously, Dr. Murray served as Principal Associate Director for Science and Technology at Lawrence Livermore National Laboratory from 2004 to 2009 and was president of the American Physical Society (APS) in 2009. Before joining Lawrence Livermore, she was Senior Vice President of Physical Sciences and Wireless Research after a 27-year-long career at Bell Laboratories Research. As an experimentalist, Dr. Murray is known for her scientific accomplishments in condensed matter and surface physics. She has published more than 70 papers in peer-reviewed journals and holds two patents in near-field optical data storage and optical display technology. Dr. Murray was elected to the National Academy of Sciences in 1999, to the American Academy of Arts and Sciences in 2001, and to the National Academy of Engineering in 2002. She has served on more than 100 national and international scientific advisory committees, governing boards and National Research Council panels and as a member of the National Commission on the BP Deepwater Horizon Oil Spill and Offshore Drilling, and she is currently chair of the National Research Council Division of Engineering and Physical Science. She received her B.S. in 1973 and her Ph.D. in physics in 1978 from the Massachusetts Institute of Technology.

Monica Olvera de la Cruz is the Lawyer Taylor Professor of Materials Science & Engineering, professor of chemistry and of chemical and biological engineering, and director of the Materials Research Center at Northwestern University. Dr. Olvera de la Cruz obtained her B.A. in physics from the Universidad Nacional Autónoma de México (UNAM) in 1981, and her Ph.D. in physics from Cambridge University, United Kingdom, in 1985. She was a guest scientist (1985-1986) at the National Institute of Standards and Technology, Gaithersburg, Maryland. From 1995-1997 she was a staff scientist in the Commissariat a l'Energie Atomique, Saclay, France, where she also held visiting scientist positions in 1993 and in 2003. She has developed theoretical models to determine the thermodynamics, statistics and dynamics of macromolecules in complex environments including multicomponent solutions of heterogeneous synthetic and biological molecules, and molecular electrolytes. She serves on the advisory boards of many national research centers and is a member of the editorial board of *Macromolecules, Journal of Polymer Science Polymer B: Polymer Physics, Current Opinion in Solid State and Materials Science,* and *Annual Review of Materials Research.* She is a member of the National Academy of Sciences and a fellow of the American Academy of Arts and Sciences.

Nicholas A. Peppas is the Fletcher Stuckey Pratt Chair in Engineering, chair of the Department of Biomedical Engineering, and professor of chemical engineering, biomedical engineering and pharmacy at the University of Texas at Austin. Dr. Peppas is a pioneer in the synthesis, characterization and dynamic behavior of polymer networks, particularly hydrogels. He is a leading researcher, inventor and pacesetter in the field of drug delivery and controlled release, a field that he helped develop into a mature area of scholarly and applied research. As an inventor of new biomaterials, he has contributed seminal work in the field of feedback-controlled biomedical devices. The multidisciplinary approach of his research in biomolecular engineering blends modern molecular and cellular biology with engineering to generate next-generation systems and devices, including bioMEMS with enhanced applicability, reliability, functionality, and longevity. His contributions have been translated into more than 20 medical products. He has received numerous awards including the Founders Award of the National Academy of Engineering (2012); the Distinguished Achievement Award from the Biomedical Engineering Society (2010); the Founders Awards of the American Institute of Chemical Engineers (AIChE), the Society for Biomaterials (SFB) and the Controlled Release Society (CRS); and the Pierre Galletti Award of the American Institute of Medical and Biological Engineering (AIMBE). He is president of the International Union of Societies of Biomaterials Science and Engineering and president-elect of the Engineering Section of the American Association for the Advancement of Science (AAAS). He is a Fellow of AAAS, ACS, APS, MRS, AIChE, AIMBE, BMES, SFB, ASEE, CRS and AAPS. Dr. Peppas is an elected member of the National Academy of Engineering (NAE), the Institute of Medicine (IOM), the National Academy of France and the Royal National Academy of Spain. A native of Athens, Greece, he received his B.S. from the National Technical University of Athens in 1971 and his Sc.D. from MIT in 1973, both in chemical engineering. He holds honorary doctorates from the Universities of Ghent, Parma, Athens, and Ljubljana.

Lynne J. Regan is professor of molecular biophysics and biochemistry, professor of chemistry, and director of the Integrated Graduate Program in Physical and Engineering Biology at Yale University. The program is designed to train a new generation of scientists skilled in applying physics and engineering methods and reasoning to biological research, while remaining sufficiently sophisticated in their biological training that they will be able to readily identify and tackle cutting-edge problems in the life sciences. Dr. Regan's research focuses on protein structure, function, and design, particularly the question of how a protein's primary sequence specifies its three-dimensional structure. Dr. Regan received a B.A. from Oxford University in 1981 and a Ph.D. from the Massachusetts Institute of Technology in 1987. She has been a Visiting Scientist at E.I. du Pont de Nemours & Company and a visitor in the Structural Studies Division of the Medical Research Council Laboratory of Molecular Biology, Cambridge, United Kingdom.

J. David Roessner is Senior Fellow with SRI International's Center for Science, Technology and Economic Development and Professor of Public Policy Emeritus at Georgia Institute of Technology. Dr. Roessner's research interests include national and regional technology policy, the evaluation of research programs, industry–university research collaboration, technology transfer, and assessment of interdisciplinary research. His recent projects include evaluations of NSF-funded U.S. Engineering Research Centers and State/Industry–University Cooperative Research Centers; estimates of the national and regional economic impact of NSF Engineering Research Centers, design of the Technology Innovation Centers Program for the King Abdulaziz City for Science and Technology (KACST), Saudi Arabia's national science and technology agency; strategic planning for a university-based innovation center at Universidad Catolica in Chile; and a review of approaches to understanding and measuring interdisciplinary research for the NSF. Dr. Roessner has written numerous technical reports and published in policy-oriented journals such as *Policy Analysis*, *Policy Sciences, Journal of Technology Transfer, Issues in Science and Technology, Research Evaluation, Scientometrics,* and *Research Policy.* Dr. Roessner also is a contributor to and editor of several books, including *Government Innovation Policy: Design, Implementation, Evaluation* (St. Martin's Press, 1988). During 2003-2008 he served as Senior Evaluation Consultant to the National Academies' Keck Futures Initiative. He holds B.S. and M.S. degrees from Brown and Stanford Universities, respectively, and a Ph.D. in Science, Technology and Public Policy from Case Western Reserve University.

Workshop on Key Challenges in the Implementation of Convergence: Agenda and Participants

AGENDA

September 16

8:00   **Welcome**
Chair: Joseph DeSimone (NAS, NAE), Committee Chair, Frank Hawkins Kenan Institute of Private Enterprise, University of North Carolina, and North Carolina State University
- Overview of the background and goals of the meeting: *Joseph DeSimone*
- Welcome on behalf of the National Academies:
  - *Ralph Cicerone (NAS), President, National Academy of Sciences*
  - *C. D. Mote, Jr. (NAE), President, National Academy of Engineering*
  - *Harvey Fineberg (IOM), President, Institute of Medicine (by video)*
- How the goals of convergence complement OSTP priorities and activities: *White House Office of Science and Technology Policy (OSTP)*

123

8:30   **Recognizing Emerging Areas of Science at the**
            Convergence Interface
            Chair: Nicholas Peppas (NAE, IOM), University of Texas at
            Austin
            Session goal: What can convergence achieve and
            what are selected examples of science with exciting
            implications that cannot be achieved without a
            convergence mindset and approach?
            • *Phillip Sharp (NAS, IOM), Massachusetts Institute of*
              Technology

9:00   **Establishing Background and Introduction to the**
            Examples of Convergent and Transdisciplinary
            Science
            Chair: Hannah Valantine, Stanford University
            Session goal: What is the existing research base on
            how to foster and measure the success of convergent,
            transdisciplinary, and/or team-science-based research?
            • Overview of NRC Study of the Science of Team
              Science: *Hannah Valantine, Stanford University*
            • Review of the committee's definition of convergence:
              Julie Thompson Klein, Wayne State University and David
              Roessner, SRI International

9:30   Break

Fostering Convergence in the Real World
How can the goals of convergence translate into practical results; that
is, what have groups and organizations specifically done to support
and foster convergence-enabled science? What has worked well and
what has not worked as well? Speakers representing several different
perspectives will provide brief snapshots of what they did, what
challenges they faced, and what they learned.

9:45   The ecosystem of convergent research and innovation
            in the life sciences: *Cherry Murray (NAS, NAE), Harvard*
            University

10:00   **Key Organizational Structures and Needs**
            Chair: Timothy Galitski, EMD Millipore Corporation and
            Institute for Systems Biology
            Session goal: Speakers in this session will particularly
            highlight factors in the successful implementation of

convergent research such as organizational policies and support structures, strategies to address differences in research practices from bringing diverse communities together, and physical and technical components.

- *Carla Shatz (NAS, IOM), Bio-X, Stanford University*
- *Anna Barker, Transformative Healthcare Networks and Complex Adaptive Systems Network, Arizona State University*
- *Susan Singer, Carleton College and National Science Foundation*

11:00 **Faculty Issues**
Chair: Cato Laurencin (NAE, IOM), University of Connecticut
Session goal: Speakers in this session will particularly focus on issues such as institutional rewards systems for convergence research and hiring, retention, promotion, and professional development of faculty

- *Fernando Martinez, Bio5 Institute, University of Arizona*
- *Donald Ingber (IOM), Wyss Institute for Biologically Inspired Engineering, Harvard University*
- *Gerald Rubin, (NAS, IOM), Janelia Farm Research Campus, Howard Hughes Medical Institute*

12:00 Working Lunch and Activity

If you could recommend *one action* each of the following actors could take that would best facilitate convergent research, what action would that be? Please try to identify a recommended action for at least two of the following categories. Write your answers on the provided post-it notes and affix them to the space beneath the name of the actor:

- a) Institutions (e.g., universities, professional associations, nonprofits)
- b) Units/Departments
- c) Principal Investigators/Team Leaders
- d) Educators
- e) Postdoctoral Fellows and Students
- f) Funding Agencies
- g) Journal Editors

1:00 **Challenges of Convergent Thinking and Innovation**
Chair: Carol Folt, University of North Carolina, Chapel Hill
- *Arunava Majumdar (NAE), Google*

Fostering Convergence in the Real World, *continued*

1:30   **Education and Training**
            Chair: Lynne Regan, Yale University
            Session goal: Speakers in this session will highlight
            issues surrounding the education and training of
            students. Issues might include ensuring students get
            the breadth of training and experience to work in a
            multidisciplinary setting but sufficient subject expertise
            for a major; how to issue degrees that span multiple
            departments or institutions; or other areas.
            • *Katerina V. Thompson, University of Maryland College
              Park*
            • *Simon Mochrie, Yale University*
            • *Andrea Stith, BioFrontiers Institute, University of
              Colorado*

2:30   **Interinstitutional Arrangements and Partnerships**
            Chair: Sharon Glotzer, University of Michigan
            Session goal: Speakers in this session will particularly
            discuss arrangements that span institutions.
            • *Bruce Walker (IOM), Ragon Institute, Massachusetts
              General Hospital, Massachusetts Institute of Technology,
              and Harvard University*
            • *David Canter, North Campus Research Complex,
              University of Michigan*
            • *Regis Kelly, California Institute for Quantitative
              Biosciences (QB3), University of California*

3:30   Brief Break and Move to Small-Group Discussion
            Sections

3:45   **Discussion Sessions**
            Session goal: Participants will be asked to think about
            the examples and models presented in the workshop
            as well as their own experiences, and start drawing
            out lessons on what works in different circumstances.
            Are there common themes? Are there factors that affect
            which model(s) appear to work best in different settings
            or for different goals? Participants will be assigned to a
            group based on their preferences and in order to get a
            balanced distribution. Discussion sessions will be given
            questions to use as starting points.

- GROUP A: Key Organizational Structures and Needs
  Chair: Robert Nerem (NAE, IOM), Georgia Institute of Technology
  Rapporteur: Adah Almutairi, University of California San Diego

- GROUP B: Faculty Issues
  Chair: Carl Simon, University of Michigan
  Rapporteur: Joshua Kritzer, Tufts University

- GROUP C: Education and Training
  Chair: Emery Brown (IOM), Massachusetts Institute of Technology
  Rapporteur: Jasmine Foo, University of Minnesota-Twin Cities

- GROUP D: Interinstitutional Arrangements and Partnerships
  Chair: Matthew Tirrell (NAE), University of Chicago
  Rapporteur: Manu Platt, Georgia Institute of Technology and Emory University

5:30   Adjourn for Day
        Reception to follow

September 17

8:15   **Introduction to Day 2**: *Joseph DeSimone, Committee Chair*

8:30   **Feedback from the Breakout Groups**
        Chair: Monica Olvera de la Cruz, Northwestern University
        Session goal: Breakout session rapporteurs will provide brief recaps of the key points from their group, followed by discussion.

9:30   **Funding Models**
        Chair: James Gentile, Hope College
        Session goal: Provide an opportunity for agencies and foundations to share how they think about this issue and what issues or challenges they face.
        - *Jon Lorsch, National Institute of General Medical Sciences, National Institutes of Health*

- *Dinah Singer, National Cancer Institute, National Institutes of Health*
- *Joann Roskoski, Directorate for Biological Sciences, National Science Foundation*
- *Maria Pellegrini, W.M. Keck Foundation*

10:30   Break

10:45   **Plenary: Roadmap for the Future**
            Discussion Leaders: Susan Hockfield, Massachusetts Institute of Technology and Joseph DeSimone, Frank Hawkins Kenan Institute of Private Enterprise, University of North Carolina, and North Carolina State University
            Session goal: A facilitated discussion to draw out key messages and lessons learned from the workshop.

12:15   Concluding Remarks: *Joseph DeSimone, Committee Chair*

12:30   **Workshop Adjourns**

PARTICIPANT LIST

Margaret Ackerman
Assistant Professor
Thayer School of Engineering
Dartmouth College

Adah Almutairi
Associate Professor
Skaggs School of Pharmacy and
    Pharmaceutical Sciences
University of California, San
    Diego

Joseph Alper
Consulting Science Writer

Adam Arkin
Dean A. Richard Newton
    Memorial Professor,
    Department of Bioengineering
University of California, Berkeley
Director, Physical Biosciences
    Division
Lawrence Berkeley National
    Laboratory

Amanda Arnold
Senior Policy Advisor
MIT Washington Office

Ann Arvin
Vice Provost and Dean of Research
Lucile Salter Packard Professor
    of Pediatrics and Professor of
    Microbiology & Immunology
Stanford University

Dennis Ausiello
Director, Center for Assessment
    Technology and Continuous
    Health
Jackson Professor of Clinical
    Medicine, Harvard Medical
    School
Chief, Department of Medicine,
    Massachusetts General
    Hospital

Randy Avent
Professor, Department of
    Computer Science
Associate Vice Chancellor for
    Research Development
North Carolina State University

Roberto Barbero
AAAS Fellow
Technology and Innovation
    Division
Office of Science and Technology
    Policy
Executive Office of the President

Anna Barker
Professor and Director,
    Transformative Healthcare
    Networks
Co-Director, Complex Adaptive
    Systems Network
Arizona State University

Cynthia Bauerle
Assistant Director
Undergraduate and Graduate
    Education
Howard Hughes Medical Institute

Ann Beheler
Executive Director of Emerging
  Technology Grants
Collin College

Rena Bizios
Peter T. Flawn Professor
Department of Biomedical
  Engineering
University of Texas at San Antonio

Krastan Blagoev
Program Director, Physics of
  Living Systems
Directorate for Mathematical &
  Physical Sciences
National Science Foundation

William B. Bonvillian
Director
MIT Washington Office

Emery Brown
Professor of Computational
  Neuroscience and Health
  Sciences and Technology
Massachusetts Institute of
  Technology
Warren M. Zapol Professor of
  Anesthesia
Harvard Medical School

David Canter
Executive Director
North Campus Research Complex
University of Michigan

Ruben Carbonell
Director
William R. Kenan, Jr. Institute for
  Engineering, Technology &
  Science
North Carolina State University

V. Celeste Carter
Program Director
Advanced Technological
  Education Program
Directorate for Education &
  Human Resources
National Science Foundation

Miyoung Chun
Executive Vice President of
  Science Programs
The Kavli Foundation

Ralph Cicerone
President
National Academy of Sciences

Lee Ann Clements
Professor of Biology and Marine
  Science
Chair, Division of Science and
  Mathematics
Jacksonville University

James Collins
William F. Warren Distinguished
  Professor
Department of Biomedical
  Engineering
Boston University

Clark Cooper
Senior Advisor for Science
  and Head of the Office of
  Multidisciplinary Activities
Directorate for Mathematical &
  Physical Sciences
National Science Foundation

Joseph DeSimone
Director, Frank Hawkins Kenan
    Institute of Private Enterprise
Chancellor's Eminent Professor
    of Chemistry, University of
    North Carolina (UNC)
William R. Kenan Jr. Distinguished
    Professor of Chemical
    Engineering, NC State
    University and of Chemistry,
    UNC

Raymond DuBois
Executive Director
Biodesign Institute
Arizona State University

Jennifer Elisseeff
Jules Stein Professor
Department of Biomedical
    Engineering and Wilmer Eye
    Institute
Johns Hopkins University

Pelagie Favi
Graduate Student
Department of Materials Science
    and Engineering
University of Tennessee

Harvey Fineberg
President
Institute of Medicine

Michael Fisher
Distinguished University
    Professor and Regents
    Professor
Institute for Physical Science and
    Technology and Department
    of Physics
University of Maryland

Carol Folt
Chancellor
University of North Carolina,
    Chapel Hill

Jasmine Foo
McKnight Land Grant Assistant
    Professor of Mathematics
University of Minnesota-Twin
    Cities

Cathy Fromen
Graduate Student
Department of Chemical
    Engineering
North Carolina State University

Timothy Galitski
Head of Science & Technology
EMD Millipore Corporation
Affiliate Professor
Institute for Systems Biology

James Gentile
Dean for the Natural and Applied
    Sciences
Hope College

Ronald Germain
Chief, Lymphocyte Biology
    Section
National Institute of Allergy and
    Infectious Diseases
National Institutes of Health

Sharon Glotzer
S. W. Churchill Collegiate
    Professor of Chemical
    Engineering
Professor of Materials Science &
    Engineering
Professor of Physics, Applied
    Physics and Macromolecular
    Science & Engineering
University of Michigan

Piotr Grodzinski
Director, Office of Cancer
    Nanotechnology Research
National Cancer Institute
National Institutes of Health

Xue Han
Assistant Professor
Department of Biomedical
    Engineering
Boston University

William Harris
President and CEO
Science Foundation Arizona

James Zachary Hilt
Associate Professor
Department of Chemical
    Engineering
University of Kentucky

Margaret Hilton
Senior Program Officer
Board on Science Education
National Research Council

Susan Hockfield
Professor of Neuroscience and
    President Emeritus
Massachusetts Institute of
    Technology

Kathryn Hughes
Senior Program Officer
Board on Chemical Sciences and
    Technology
National Research Council

Lynn Hull
AAAS Science and Technology
    Policy Fellow
Office of Cancer Nanotechnology
    Research
National Cancer Institute
National Institutes of Health

Donald Ingber
Director, Wyss Institute for
    Biologically Inspired
    Engineering
Judah Folkman Professor of
    Vascular Biology, Harvard
    Medical School & Boston
    Children's Hospital
Professor of Bioengineering
Harvard University

Ravi Iyengar
Professor and Chair, Department
    of Pharmacology and Systems
    Therapeutics
Director, Experimental
    Therapeutics Institute
Icahn School of Medicine at
    Mount Sinai

Thomas Kalil
Deputy Director for Technology
    and Innovation
Technology and Innovation
    Division
Office of Science and Technology
    Policy
Executive Office of the President

Lydia Kavraki
Noah Harding Professor of
    Computer Science and
    Bioengineering
Rice University

Rusty Kelley
Program Officer
Burroughs Wellcome Fund

Regis Kelly
Director
California Institute for
    Quantitative Biosciences (QB3)

Melissa Kinney
Graduate Student
Parker H. Petit Institute for
    Bioengineering & Bioscience
Georgia Institute of Technology

Joshua Kritzer
Assistant Professor of Chemistry
Tufts University

Joerg Lahann
Director, Biointerfaces Institute
University of Michigan

Cato Laurencin
Wilda Van Dusen Distinguished
    Professor of Orthopaedic
    Surgery
Professor of Chemical, Materials
    and Biomolecular Engineering
CEO, Connecticut Institute for
    Clinical and Translational
    Science
Director, Institute for Regenerative
    Engineering
University of Connecticut

Jerry Lee
Deputy Director
Center for Strategic Scientific
    Initiatives
National Cancer Institute
National Institutes of Health

Jon R. Lorsch
Director
National Institute of General
    Medical Sciences
National Institutes of Health

Gesham Magombedze
Postdoctoral Fellow
National Institute for
    Mathematical and Biological
    Synthesis (NIMBioS)
University of Tennessee

Arun Majumdar
Director of Energy Initiatives
Google.org

Fernando Martinez
Director, BIO5 Institute
University of Arizona

Marcia K. McNutt
Editor in Chief, *Science*
American Association for the
    Advancement of Science

William Miller
Program Director
Directorate for Biological Sciences
National Science Foundation

Adrienne Minerick
Associate Professor
Department of Chemical
    Engineering
Michigan Technological University

Martha Mitchell
Associate Dean of Research
College of Engineering
New Mexico State University

Simon Mochrie
Professor of Physics and Applied
    Physics
Yale University

C.D. Mote, Jr.
President
National Academy of Engineering

Kelly Moynihan
Graduate Student
Department of Biological
    Engineering
Massachusetts Institute of
    Technology

Sarah Mueller
Graduate Student
University of North Carolina at
    Chapel Hill

Cherry Murray
Dean
School of Engineering and
    Applied Sciences
Harvard University

Larry Nagahara
Director, Office of Physical
    Sciences-Oncology
National Cancer Institute
National Institutes of Health

Eric Nawrocki
Bioinformatics Specialist
Janelia Farm Research Campus
Howard Hughes Medical Institute

Robert Nerem
Parker H. Petit Distinguished
    Chair for Engineering in
    Medicine and Institute
    Professor Emeritus
Former Director, Parker H. Petit
    Institute for Bioengineering
    and Bioscience
Georgia Institute of Technology

Corey O'Hern
Associate Professor
Departments of Mechanical
    Engineering & Materials
    Science and Physics
Yale University

Monica Olvera de la Cruz
Lawyer Taylor Professor of
    Materials Science and
    Engineering
Director, Materials Research
    Center
Northwestern University

Maria Pellegrini
Executive Director of Programs
W. M. Keck Foundation

Nicholas Peppas
Fletcher Stuckey Pratt Chair in
    Engineering
Chair, Department of Biomedical
    Engineering
Professor, Departments of
    Chemical Engineering,
    Biomedical Engineering and
    College of Pharmacy
University of Texas at Austin

James Petersson
Assistant Professor
Department of Chemistry
University of Pennsylvania

Roderick Pettigrew
Director
National Institute of Biomedical
    Imaging and Bioengineering
National Institutes of Health

Rember Pieper
Associate Professor,
J. Craig Venter Institute

Manu Platt
Assistant Professor
Wallace H. Coulter Department of
    Biomedical Engineering
Georgia Institute of Technology

Manu Prakash
Assistant Professor
Department of Bioengineering
Stanford University

Lynne Regan
Professor
Departments of Molecular
    Biophysics & Biochemistry
    and Chemistry
Yale University

Proctor Reid
Program Director
National Academy of Engineering

Gary Reiness
Associate Dean of the College of
    Arts and Sciences;
Professor of Biology
Lewis & Clark College

Sandra Robinson
Graduate Student
Department of Biology
University of Massachusetts
    Amherst

David Roessner
Senior Fellow
Center for Science, Technology,
    and Economic Development
SRI International

Joann Roskoski
Deputy Assistant Director
Directorate for Biological Sciences
National Science Foundation

Gerald Rubin
Executive Director
Janelia Farm Research Campus
Howard Hughes Medical Institute

Pamela J. Schofield
Manager, Corporate Research &
    Development
The Procter & Gamble Company

Belinda Seto
Deputy Director
National Institute of Biomedical
    Imaging and Bioengineering
National Institutes of Health

Armon Sharei
Graduate Student
Department of Chemical
    Engineering
Massachusetts Institute of
    Technology

Phillip Sharp
Institute Professor
Koch Institute for Integrative
    Cancer Research
Massachusetts Institute of
    Technology

Lindsey Sharpe
Graduate Student
Cockrell School of Engineering
University of Texas at Austin

Carla J. Shatz
Director, Bio-X
Professor of Biology and
  Neurobiology
Stanford University

Kamal Shukla
Program Director, Molecular
  Biophysics
Directorate for Biological Sciences
National Science Foundation

Carl Simon
Founding Director, Center for the
  Study of Complex Systems
Professor of Mathematics,
  Economics, and Public Policy
University of Michigan

Dinah Singer
Head, Molecular Regulation
  Section
Director, Division of Cancer
  Biology
National Cancer Institute
National Institutes of Health

Susan Singer
Laurence McKinley Gould
  Professor
Departments of Biology and
  Cognitive Science
Carleton College
Director, Division of
  Undergraduate Education
National Science Foundation

Daniel Solomon
Dean, College of Sciences
North Carolina State University

Nelson Spruston
Scientific Program Director and
  Laboratory Head
Janelia Farm Research Campus
Howard Hughes Medical Institute

Stephanie Steichen
Graduate Student
Cockrell School of Engineering
University of Texas at Austin

Andrea L. Stith
Assistant Director for
  Interdisciplinary Education
BioFrontiers Institute
University of Colorado

Umesh Thakkar
U.S. Government Accountability
  Office

Katerina Thompson
Director
Undergraduate Research and
  Internship Programs
College of Computer,
  Mathematical, and Natural
  Sciences
University of Maryland College
  Park

Julie Thompson Klein
Professor of Humanities; and
English Department Faculty
  Fellow for Interdisciplinary
  Development
Wayne State University

Matthew Tirrell
Pritzker Director
Institute for Molecular
    Engineering
University of Chicago

Robert Tjian
President
Howard Hughes Medical Institute

Hannah Valantine
Senior Associate Dean for
    Diversity and Leadership
Professor of Cardiovascular
    Medicine
Stanford University School of
    Medicine

Amy Cheng Vollmer
Professor of Biology
Swarthmore College

Geoffrey von Maltzen
New Venture Principal
Flagship Ventures

Evan Vosburgh
Executive Director
Raymond and Beverly Sackler
    Foundation

Vivek Wadhwa
Vice President of Innovation and
    Research
Singularity University

Bruce Walker
Director
Ragon Institute of MGH, MIT and
    Harvard

Tina Winters
Associate Program Officer
Board on Behavioral, Cognitive,
    and Sensory Sciences
National Research Council

Jodi Yellin
Director, Group on Graduate
    Research and Education
Association of American Medical
    Colleges

Dorothy Zolandz
Deputy Director
Division on Earth and Life Studies
National Research Council

Board on Life Sciences Staff

Frances Sharples
Director
Board on Life Sciences
National Research Council
fsharples@nas.edu

Katherine Bowman
Senior Program Officer
Board on Life Sciences
National Research Council
kbowman@nas.edu

Carl Anderson
Program Associate
Board on Life Sciences
National Research Council
cganderson@nas.edu

Ayesha Ahmed
Senior Program Assistant
Board on Life Sciences
National Research Council
sahmed@nas.edu